BECOMING
KNOWLEDGE
FOCUSED

A PRACTICAL APPROACH
TO MANAGING KNOWLEDGE
IN INTERNATIONAL ORGANIZATIONS
by Ugochukwu N. Ugbor, Ph.D.

ISBN 978-3-9502550-1-0 (PB)

Published by the Knowledge Management Associates GmbH
for the Center for International Knowledge Management
Gersthofer Strasse 162, A-1180 Vienna, Austria
office@c-ikm.org

This book is a part of the
Becoming Knowledge Focused series
of reviewed articles and books

For my brilliant daughters Melissa and Michelle

TABLE OF CONTENTS

LIST OF FIGURES

LIST OF TABLES

FOREWORD

Revolution, according to Merriam-Webster's dictionary [1], is "a sudden, radical or complete change … a basic reorientation". To diplomats and international civil servants, the changes surrounding us are not mere trends, but workings of large, unruly forces: globalization, which has opened new challenges and possibilities in international affairs. The spread of information technology, the improved computer networks, the breaking-up of the former Soviet Union, the politically charged reform proposals and reductions of international organizations budgets [2]—partly a consequence of the rise of the Neo-Conservative movement [3] among powerful Western governments—are all part of the new economy, also known as the Information Age. The fundamental sources of relevance for organizations are now "knowledge and communications" [4].

Although KM and implementation strategies have been researched in knowledge intensive firms (KIFs), like business consultancies [5], and in various other for-profit organizations [6], we know little about the KM in international organizations. This research will attempt to fill this gap, by investigating how knowledge is managed in various such organizations.

As further research is done to help international organizations function more effectively from the political and governing share [7-12], it is important to understand the interrelations between the different variables at play at lower levels and to explore whether prior research in areas of management and technology may provide adequate pointers. The goal of the research, therefore, is to take a step in that direction by systematically analysing knowledge and its management in international organizations (cf. Chapter 1), and linking current issues facing international organizations (cf. Chapter 2) to a rich tradition in knowledge management (cf. Chapter 3) that can help identify potential organizational solutions to increase efficiency and effectiveness (cf. Chapter 4). While the functions of international organizations are known [13, 14], the unique contribution of this research lies in the clarification of the interconnections between the functions of international organizations and knowledge, and the development of a practical approach to becoming knowledge focused.

PREFACE

The globalization of political, economic and cultural processes has created the awareness that some problems need to be solved on a worldwide basis. Given that governance is a continual process in which problems are identified and solved, this has led many theorists and practitioners to propose reforms [7, 12, 15-18] to help international organizations keep pace with their environment and achieve their goals.

It must be noted that much of the complex and inefficient machinery of international organizations results from deep political and cultural differences, the divisions between political and economic interests of nations and regions—particularly the chasms between the rich and the poor [19] and the powerful and the powerless [20]. Inefficiencies arguably lie beneath the political and bureaucratic sphere, including issues surrounding Knowledge Management (KM) and intellectual capital deployment [21].

This book does not claim to address efficiency matters from the political or governing sphere, nor does it propose specific programmatic changes to work of international organizations; rather it presents a pragmatic "bottom-up" approach, based on case studies and interviews conducted at a number of international organizations. The relevance of this approach emerges from the verification that the efficiency gains achieved through reform or restructuring processes in an international organization can go only as far as the organization's operational efficiency allows [7]:

> *The constraints here are serious and must give cause for concern... Here and there throughout the system there are offices and units collecting the information available, but there is no group [or practice of]... constantly monitoring the present operation, learning from experience, grasping at all that science and technology has to offer, launching new ideas and methods, challenging established practices, and provoking thought inside and outside the system. Deprived of such a vital stimulus, it is obvious that the best use cannot be made of the sources available.... Its absence may well be the greatest constraint of all...*

At the organizational level, the ceiling for improvements is set by the system's ability to leverage the skills and talents of its staff [13], as well as the capacities of its member countries. It is from this standpoint that the ideas contained in this research have been developed. This is a humble thesis, which does not intend to reinvent the wheel. Quite the contrary, it attempts to devise a practical approach to managing knowledge that takes stock of the intellectual capital resources and normative and operational functions of international organizations.

I sincerely hope that the ideas in this research will help to spark some interest and, above all, action to reinvigorate the functions of international organizations by the strategic management of knowledge.

ACKNOWLEDGEMENTS

Special thanks to Prof. Dr. Ina Wagner, Head of the Institute for Technology Assessment and Design, Vienna University of Technology, Austria and Prof. Dr. Carlos Chanduvi, Open University Business School, UK and Dr. Andreas Brandner, CEO Knowledge Management Associates as well as many others who have inspired confidence in me by validating the importance of my research including Dr. Kandeh Yumkella, Director General, UNIDO, Mr. Robert Workman, Head Nuclear Knowledge Management, IAEA, Mr Vincent Job, Director, Information and Communication Technologies (ICT), IMO, Dr. David Skyrme, Founder and President, David Skyrme Associates, UK, Prof. Dr. Nigel Kermode, Open University, UK, Prof. Dr. Klaus Tochtermann, Graz University of Technology, Austria, Director, Know-Center, Graz and Prof. Dr. Stefano Armandi, International University Vienna.

I am enormously grateful to the many institutional leaders and managers who generously volunteered their time to be interviewed. This project stands on the shoulders of these "giants", whose combined ideas are what have made this research possible.

CHAPTER 1 INTERNATIONAL ORGANIZATIONS

In order to fully appreciate the term "international organization", it would be necessary to reflect on some historic factors that have led to its meaning before concentrating on the meaning in the context of this research. The concept of international organization can be traced as far back as the writings of Dante, the 14th century poet and writer, who envisioned a "universal man" and the "world state" [22]. In the context of modern nation state systems relations, its roots can be found in the writings of Emanuel Kant [23] who proposed a "league of peace" among "free states". However, the League of Nations did not become an identifiable entity until the 1920s, following the First World War. The academic inquiry that followed was often termed "idealistic" as they were concerned with questions about "should" and "ought" [24].

After the Second World War, and following the creation of the United Nations in 1954, the study of and interest in international organizations took a more "realistic" perspective with a focus on "state sovereignty, the elements of national power, military strategy, diplomacy and other instruments of statecraft" [24]. Thus, the realist perspective was relegated mainly to an international organization's necessity for "managing the balance of power", as opposed to a more grandiose global world view, like creating larger communities beyond nation states—as idealists had formerly suggested since the inception of the concept.

Over the next ten to twenty years [in the 1950s and 1960s] of the post war era, the vision of both idealists and realists started to fade, along with the distinction between them, to include broader concepts beyond the United Nations. Organizations concerned with regional security issues started to be called international organizations. Organizations like the European Coal and Steel Community (ECSC), the Arab League, the North Atlantic Treaty Organization (NATO), and so on.

In the 1970s and 1980s, the concept of an international organization faced another paradigm shift. World economies became more intricately interdependent [25] and, as a result, a global consciousness emerged, especially after the oil embargo in 1973 [26]. The globalist perspective stressed the intricate and complex interdependencies between national governments beyond war and peace, including economic and other issues that did not lend themselves to resolution through force. The "globalist" view further enlarged the concept of the international organization, traditionally associated with intergovernmental organizations, to include other actors influencing world politics, including non-governmental organizations and even multinational organizations and others:

> ... *the overwhelming evidence points to the conclusion that we are entering into a basically new arrangement of international political issues, policy.and actors ... a sharply growing volume of transnational policymaking involves sub-national political units, national political units non-state actors, such as multinational corporations and transnational elite groups, and officials of regional and global international organizations...*
> [27p. xxi]

INTERGOVERNMENTAL ORGANIZATIONS

For the purpose of this book, the term is neither a non-governmental organization, nor a multinational organization, but it is the "union of nations, established or recognized by them for the purpose of realizing a common end" [28], "… created by multilateral treaty or agreement among states…"[29]. It is "a formal arrangement transcending national boundaries that provides for the establishment of institutional machinery to facilitate cooperation among members in the security, economic, social or related fields" [30]. Thus, international organizations used here refer solely to inter-governmental organizations with member countries. For example, the UN, EU and OPEC. In this regard, an international organization exists to serve its sovereign member states and related industries.

1.1   INTERNATIONAL ORGANIZATIONS STAKEHOLDERS

Stakeholders have an impact on the purpose of the organization [31] (cf. Section 4.2). Here we consider who the stakeholders of international organizations are. The diagram in this section (Figure 1.1) does not attempt to represent a bureaucratic or organizational structure, but provide a high-level understanding of the nature of relationships that exist in these organizations. Evidence was generated from interviews, international organization websites and published literature on international organizations. Therefore, Figure 1.1 presents a simplified stakeholder diagram where internal stakeholders are seen as the organization's employees (management and staff), and external stakeholders as the bureaucratic policy organs and other groups.

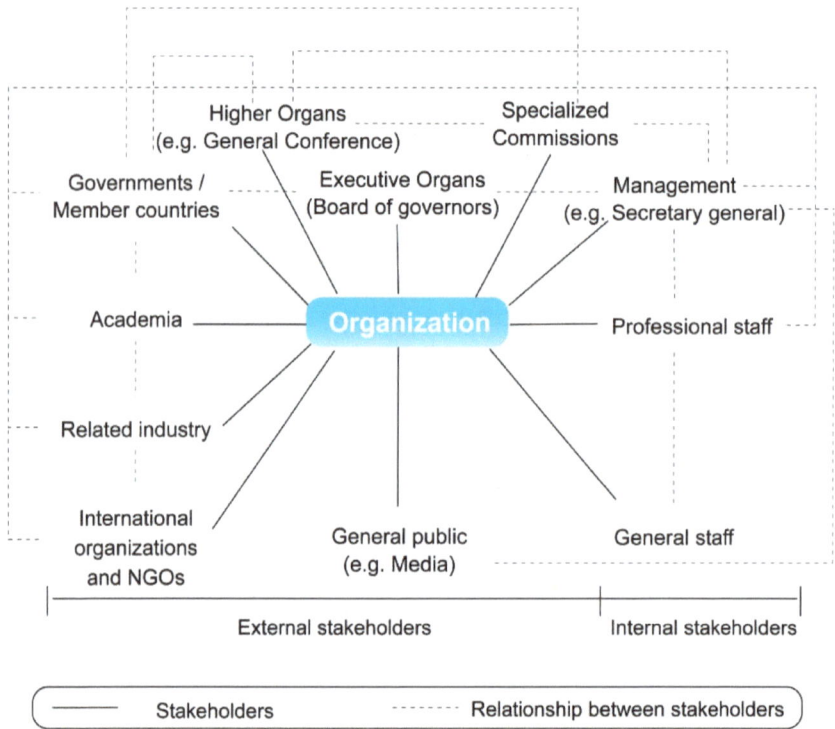

Figure 1.1: International organizations stakeholder diagram

1.2   THE ROLE OF INTERNATIONAL ORGANIZATIONS

It is important to understand how intergovernmental organizations' functions have evolved in relation to the changing global landscape, particularly with regard to the debate around international organizations' operational and normative functions. Evidence on the classification is drawn from published literature and various public documents, including the international organizations' websites.

1.2.1   NORMATIVE FUNCTIONS

Normative functions are intended to influence the perceptions of actors in the international community within a specified set of issues [13], while implementation is left to an organization's stakeholders [28]—

specifically its member countries. Such international organizations function mainly through forums for debate on issues of economic and political significance, setting targets and monitoring the performance of member countries vis-à-vis their regulatory mandate. For example, the International Maritime Organization (IMO) is responsible for over 40 international conventions and agreements related to maritime safety and environmental standards. The treaty on non-proliferation of nuclear weapons (NPT) established a safeguard system under the responsibility of the International Atomic Energy Agency (IAEA), which also plays a central role in nuclear technology transfer for peaceful purposes. The United Nations Office on Drugs and Crime (UNODC) is responsible for developing and implementing treaties and conventions related to drugs crime and terrorism. Similarly, the Organization of the Petroleum Exporting Countries (OPEC) was established to help co-ordinate and unify the petroleum policies of its members [32].

1.2.2   OPERATIONAL FUNCTIONS

Operational functions involve the implementation in recipient countries of decisions made by participating governments [33]. Whilst many normative international organizations have an operational component, some international organizations with operational functions have no formal regulatory mandate, and as such they provide consultancy services and implementation assistance for their members. For example, the work of the United Nations Industrial Development Organization (UNIDO) is focused on three broad thematic priorities [34]: poverty reduction, building trade capacity and energy and environmental concerns. The Organization for Security and Co-operation in Europe (OSCE) is another example of a operational-oriented organization, concerned with security issues, ranging from the politico-military to the socio-economic dimension [35].

1.2.3   ORGANIZATIONAL ORIENTATION

In international organizations, policy advice and governance can be both a normative and operational function, "...in the sense that it can be the last in the series of normative functions, and the first in a sequence of operational functions..."[14] For example, the global programme on maritime port security is a technical assistance response in the International Maritime Organization (IMO) to developing countries' needs to upgrade infrastructure and training to meet several regulatory standards of the Safety of Life at Sea (SOLAS) conventions (cf. Section 2.4). The two functions (normative and operational) are mutually supportive. However, OPEC, a normative oriented organization (in Figure 1.2), does not have an operational component, in that sense that is not directly involved in oil production capacity building. Oil production capacity is left solely to the independent purview of its member countries.

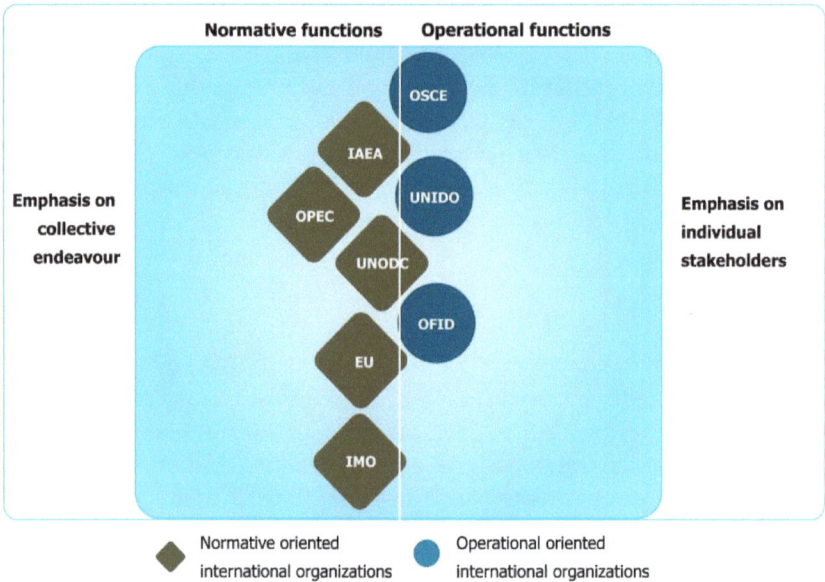

Figure 1.2: Organizational orientation

1.3   ORGANIZATIONAL ORIENTATION AND KNOWLEDGE

Blackler [36] proposed that different types of organizations depend on five different types of knowledge--embrained, embodied, encultured, embedded and encoded knowledge.

Embrained knowledge depends on the conceptual skills and cognitive abilities of workers, used to solving novel problems. Emphasis is on contributions of key individuals in innovative organizations dependent on embrained knowledge. **Embodied** knowledge is action-oriented and rooted in specific physical context, and emphasis is on the contributions of key specialized individuals. **Encultured** knowledge is dependent on communication and collaboration of members. It emphasizes creativity and uniqueness in problem solving, and is dependent on collaboration between client and agent networks. **Embedded** knowledge resides in systemic routines, procedures and technologies. The emphasis is on collective endeavour to reach solve specified issues.

Encoded knowledge is information conveyed by signs and symbols, affecting the other types of knowledge, depending on those that have adequate knowledge to decode meaning from the externalized symbols. Boundary objects as described in Star and Griesemer [37] are some examples of encoded knowledge. The term boundary objects thus refers to a broad range of artefacts that "are plastic enough to adapt to local needs and constraints of several parties employing them, yet robust enough to maintain a common identity across sites" [37 p. 393]. Some examples of boundary objects include design drawings, physical prototypes and standardized reporting forms [37]. Technologies such as Enterprise Resource Planning (ERP) systems and document archives are also considered to be boundary objects by some researchers [38-40].

In the context of international organizations' functions, all knowledge types are present, although in varying degrees, based on the orientation of the organization (cf. Figure 1.2). The operational functions of international organizations require them to share the problem of implementing policy decisions. The knowledge processing load [41], therefore, focuses on novel problem-solving, requiring a larger degree of embodied, encultured and embrained knowledge. Problem-solving in technical co-operation projects carried out by international organizations is not standardized, requiring the direct contributions of key technical specialists (embodied knowledge), communications and collaboration with stakeholders (encultured knowledge), and the creative ability of experts (embrained knowledge).

Normative functions depend more on established research knowledge (embedded knowledge), intended to influence the perceptions of international actors within a specified set of issues [13], while implementation is left to member countries [28].

1.3.1   KM IN BUSINESS VERSUS KM IN INTERNATIONAL ORGANIZATIONS

The application of KM expertise in the business sector to international organizations is not straightforward and has not been very successful [42]--only 2 of 17 international organizations surveyed reported "successful" results.

KM in businesses is generally driven by two factors: one is the competitive advantage that can be derived from knowledge [4], and the other is the developments in information technology [43]. However, KM in international organizations can be driven by more complex factors. Firstly, there is a difference in the success criteria. While companies are established to generate tangible shareholder benefits, like profits and market share, international organizations are established to help generate intangible benefits for its various stakeholders, like promoting national and regional interests specifically and to improve international cooperation in general [44-46].

Secondly, companies have a quicker feedback loop in the form of markets and profits. This makes them strive for increased efficiency [47]. International organizations lack these kinds of short feedback loops—international agreements are made for long-term benefit. For example, the United Nations Millennium Development Goals (MDG)[45] aims to secure peace and development, by vanquishing poverty, ignorance and preventable diseases. Furthermore, countries have exclusivity in official representatives at the governing sphere of international organizations, making the environment in which they operate abstract, impersonal and complex, rendering measurement of intangibles of international cooperation more difficult to articulate, locate and measure.

Thirdly, processes in the business sector are organized in order to achieve some concrete targets (like profit, or market share, and so on) at the end [47]. However, processes and functions in international organizations are not instruments to an end, but have importance in themselves. For example, international conventions and treaties are important in themselves, even before countries ratify their proposals— the Kyoto Protocol [48], remains an important objective, even though not all countries have ratified it.

Fourthly effectiveness in terms of stakeholder benefits is more important than efficiency in international organizations. In the business sector, a guiding principle is efficiency in resource utilization (i.e. productivity) [47]. In international organizations, certain inefficiencies are necessarily built into the system through the diplomatic, political and bureaucratic forces of the system [13]—For example, the insistence principle of equality [44] and the absence of intergovernmental agreements and coordination [7]. Moreover effectiveness in international organizations comprises two broad overlapping ideas [49], depending on its functions. For normative functions, an international organization is effective to the extent that its members abide by its norms and rules. For operational functions, it is effective to the extent that it achieves the objectives for which it was intended.

These major differences between businesses and international organizations influence the application of extant knowledge management. In the business sector, knowledge has instrumental value, which is directly applied to particular products and/or services. In international organizations, knowledge has a more general application. It is often used indirectly, for normative and operational functions (cf. Section 1.2), such as enabling the international community to react to changes in geopolitics, reaching common consensus on issues of global governance, and for providing services to enable countries meet internationally agreed standards.

1.3.2   APPLICATION OF KM WITHIN INTERNATIONAL ORGANIZATIONS

International organizations around the world have embraced knowledge and learning as part of their long-term vision, articulated in the report published by the Chief Executive Board (CEB) of the UN System [21]. The Committee on Program and Operational Questions (CCPOQ), an inter-agency coordination body of the United Nations system[1] presented a report [42] consisting of results of a recent survey on KM in the UN System, prepared by the World Bank (WB), in collaboration with the American Productivity and Quality Centre (APQC).   The report showed that KM is at an early stage in international organizations; that KM efforts are led mostly by

---

[1] Since October 2001, the inter-agency activities of CCPOQ are carried out by the High-Level Committee on Programs (HLCP) http://ceb.unsystem.org/Former.ACC/ccpoq.htm

information technology, (instead of supported by it as ideally is the case [50]).

The main drawbacks to the report [42] include the generality of its findings. It tries to cover "everything" about managing knowledge in every type of international organization, without first considering the organization's context and mandate. Nor does it provide evidence on links between cause and effect—why KM has failed to live up to expectations in these organizations. Furthermore, the actions recommended in the United Nations system KM report [42] addressed very broad goals, set in the 1997 UN Statement on Universal Access to Basic Communication and Information Services [51, 52], a statement emphasizing general importance of ICT to international organizations and its member countries, and particularly for least-developed countries with poor infrastructure. The statement, however, does not go as far as to recommend actions to address the internal dynamics of KM in international organizations.

The output of this research is expected to help international organizations develop a more comprehensive understanding of the process of KM and how KM can address their situation, while taking advantage of investments in KM systems (KMS). Knowledge audits in the form of interviews, developed as part of the study, helped understand contextual issues facing international organizations and the strategic KM systems proposed and implemented. The false assumptions in KMS implementation [50] regarding contingencies of IT alone as the only determinant in KM were validated through this work–or in the words of Zack and McKenny [53]:

> *The strategic advantage associated with these technologies [for KM] will not derive from having the technical skills to evaluate and implement communication technologies (or even be the first mover), but rather will come from having the appropriate social context, norms politics, reward systems and leadership to take advantage of electronic communication technology*

1.3.3   TOWARDS A CONCEPTUAL DEFINITION OF KM IN INTERNATIONAL ORGANIZATIONS

KM has received enormous attention from academia, but despite the broad interest, many different ideas still exist, some of which are shown below (Table 1.1).

Table 1.1: Definitions of KM

Hedlund [54]:	Davenport [55]:	Swan *et al.* [56]:
KM addresses the generation, representation, storage, transfer, transformation, application, embedding and protection of organizational knowledge	KM is the process of increasing the efficiency of knowledge markets by generating codifying, coordinating, and transferring knowledge	KM is about harnessing the intellectual and social capital of individuals, in order to improve organizational learning capabilities.

Two of the definitions of KM above [54, 55] follow knowledge through stages of its life cycle [43]. Following this arrangement, Alavi and Leidner [57] conclude that a minimum of four generic KM stages can be identified: creating, storing/retrieving, transferring, and applying knowledge. This framework has the disadvantage that it does not show where areas of KM research might be lacking [43]. For example, it does not seek to understand the raison d'être for KM itself. For this reason some have described such definitions as "a solution without a cause" and warned against KM becoming just another management fad [41, 58].   In an insightful paper, Zack [41] wonders: "If managing knowledge is the solution, then what is the problem?"

Sveiby [59] argues against the term "knowledge management", preferring instead the term "knowledge focused" because knowledge is a human faculty that increases individual (and consequentially organizations) capacity to act, not something that can be "managed", except by the individual him/herself cooperatively. Sveiby [59] argues that a "knowledge focused" manager looks to manage the environment in which knowledge is created and consumed, by focusing on intangibles (or intellectual capital). Likewise in international organizations, managing knowledge cannot be simplified to the four generic stages of KM [57] alone, (including creating, storing/retrieving, transferring, and applying knowledge), but managing knowledge includes managing the intangibles (or intellectual capital) inherent in the context in which international organizations operate.

International organizations' intellectual capital comprises of its member countries at the macro level, and individual specialists within and beyond the organizations boundaries at the micro level, working towards better international cooperation and collaboration. Thus, this research extends the concept of KM to include the process of managing knowledge in international organizations as defined below:

> *Managing knowledge in international organizations is about harnessing the intellectual and social capital of its member countries, and the international knowledge worker, in order to improve organizational learning, international co-operation and global governance by providing knowledge focused process perspective to achieving the organization's goals.*

1.4   INTELLECTUAL CAPITAL OF INTERNATIONAL ORGANIZATIONS

Studies of KM literature can perhaps most systematically be reviewed through a classification based on the intellectual capital (IC) of international organizations, a term used to denote the resources that drive value for an organization, including knowledge and intangibles. Like longer established concepts such as intellectual property (IP), the term intellectual capital puts human knowledge to the fore. The basic idea is that knowledge held by organizations is an asset that represents capital. Analogous to the concept of financial capital, IC is a much broader term that includes all accumulated resources that can be deployed to produce value for an organization.

Stewart's [60] three main constructs that encompass the phenomenon of IC include human capital (the talent base of the employees), structural capital (the non-human storehouses of information), and customer capital (the knowledge embedded in business networks). Other IC researchers, such as [61-63], have proposed a multifaceted description, comprising human, structural, customer, relational, and social capital.

Due to the fact that international organizations are generally non-profit making, they do not have customers in the traditional sense, thus this category has been omitted for clarity in Figure 1.3. Furthermore, since relational and social capital are intertwined [64] this book shall use both terms interchangeably. Figure 1.3 below depicts a generic IC map for international organizations, using the above constructs.

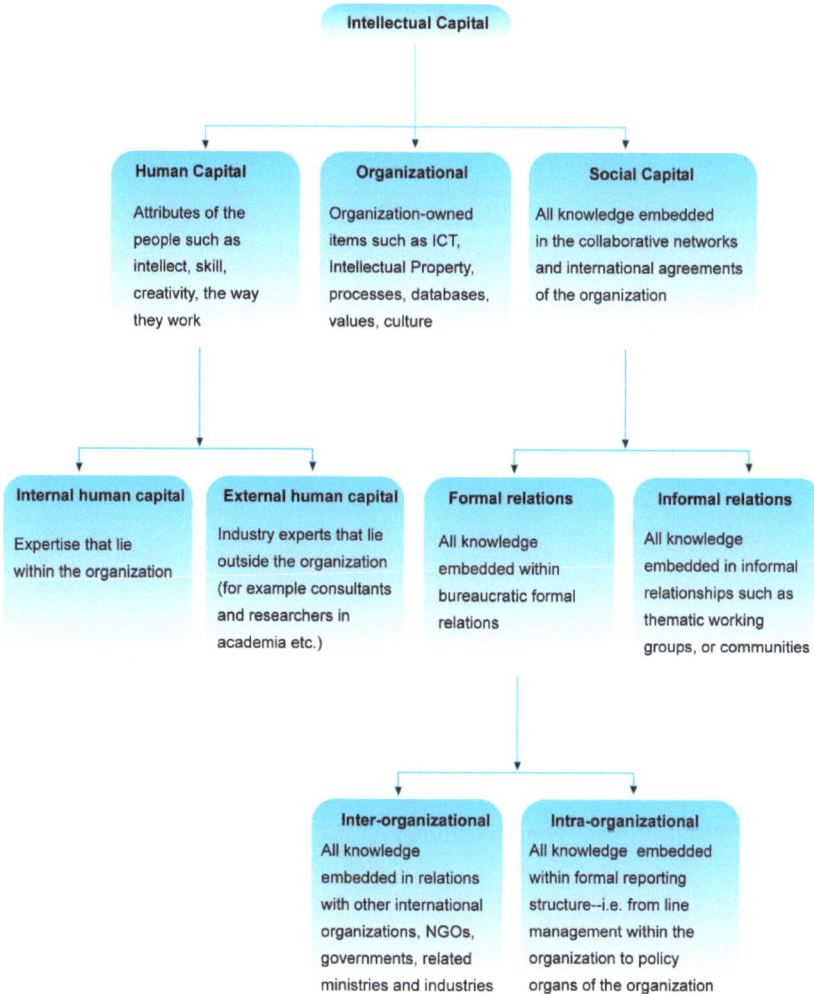

```
                         ┌─────────────────────┐
                         │ Intellectual Capital │
                         └─────────────────────┘
```

Human Capital

Attributes of the people such as intellect, skill, creativity, the way they work

Organizational

Organization-owned items such as ICT, Intellectual Property, processes, databases, values, culture

Social Capital

All knowledge embedded in the collaborative networks and international agreements of the organization

Internal human capital

Expertise that lie within the organization

External human capital

Industry experts that lie outside the organization (for example consultants and researchers in academia etc.)

Formal relations

All knowledge embedded within bureaucratic formal relations

Informal relations

All knowledge embedded in informal relationships such as thematic working groups, or communities

Inter-organizational

All knowledge embedded in relations with other international organizations, NGOs, governments, related ministries and industries

Intra-organizational

All knowledge embedded within formal reporting structure--i.e. from line management within the organization to policy organs of the organization

Figure 1.3: Generic categories of intellectual capital for international organizations

1.4.1   HUMAN CAPITAL

Human capital refers to the competence, intellectual agility and attitudes of employees—knowledge—that are used in the value creation process [65]. These resources are, by definition, not owned by the organization, and, if nurtured, can create increasing returns [66, 67]. The following highlights the intangible aspects of human capital and its management from literature. This includes dimensions of knowledge, (tacit/explicit and knowledge types) and the process of externalization and integration of knowledge.

KNOWLEDGE: TACIT/EXPLICIT

Polanyi [68] argued that all knowledge had a tacit dimension, making no epistemological dichotomy of tacit-explicit. Cook and Brown [69] concur with Polanyi's view, explaining that codified (explicit) knowledge can only be understood within a context where tacit knowledge is brought to bear. More recent discussions by Nonaka et al [70] and by Cook and Brown [69], suggest that knowledge can be both tacit and explicit. Knowledge management systems (KMS) typically focus on explicit knowledge [43], but increasing attention is being given to how KMS might support tacit knowledge embedded in social relations [50].

KM PROCESS

Nonaka et al (2000) presents four steps in this process of knowledge conversion, with an emphasis on collaborative work, known as the socialization, externalization, combination and internalization (SECI) model. This model, particularly the concept of knowledge "externalization", is useful for understanding KM.

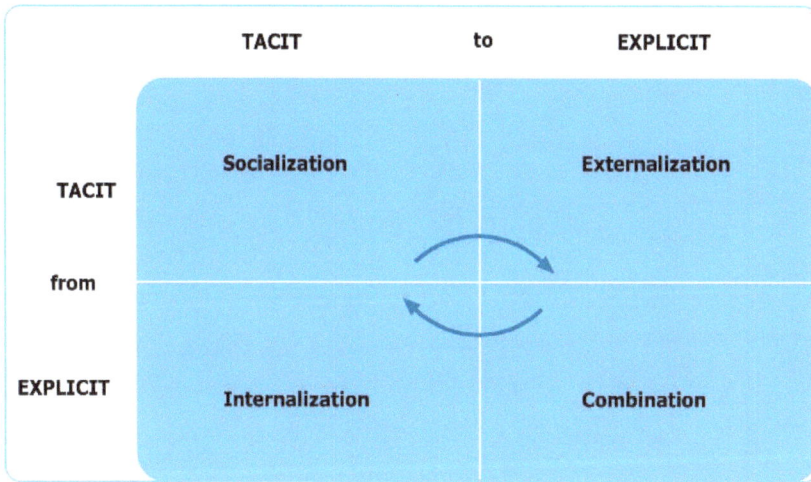

Figure 1.4: Four modes of knowledge conversion [Source: 71]

KNOWLEDGE "EXTERNALIZATION"

The second phase of Nonaka's SECI model (Figure 1.4) is externalization (tacit to explicit) where a community member's tacit knowledge is converted into an explicit form. However, there is a debate surrounding the process of "externalization" presented by Nonaka et al (2000). Cook and Brown [69] argue that knowledge cannot be "converted". They argue that organizations are better understood if explicit, tacit, individual and group knowledge are treated as "four distinct and coequal forms of knowledge, each doing work the others cannot". In their view, explicit knowledge and tacit knowledge (knowing) are seen as mutually enabling and not dichotomous. While tacit knowledge cannot be "converted", it can serve as an aid to producing and comprehending explicit knowledge (cf. Figure 1.5).

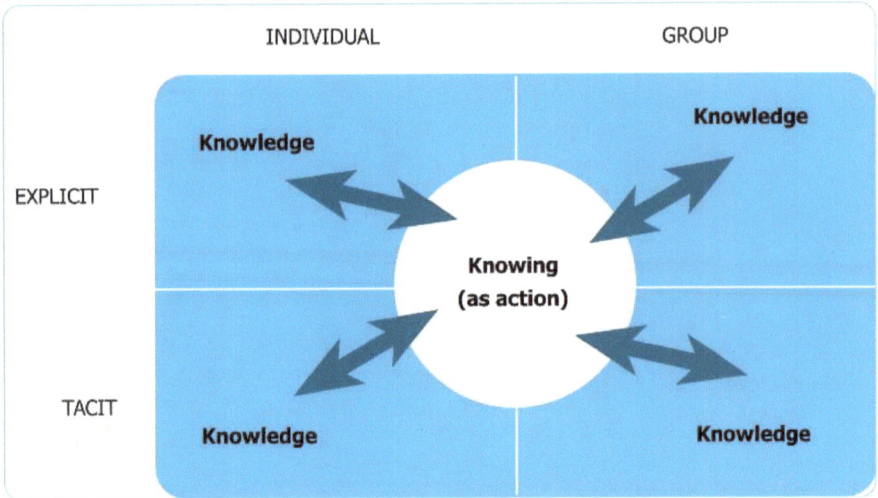

Figure 1.5: Knowledge and knowing. Bridging Epistemologies [Source: 69]

KNOWLEDGE WORK

The term knowledge work carries two different connotations in literature. On the one hand knowledge workers are defined as a distinctive subsection of the workforce. They have special skills education and professional expertise [72].

On the other one can relate knowledge work to the paradigm shift in the economies [4, 73] from largely agricultural to post industrial. A growing part of the post industrial age work is now less labour intensive or even capital intensive, but, rather, knowledge intensive in character.

The most important raw material for knowledge work is therefore information [4] and associated skills (know-how) to transform it to something of value to the organization [69] [74]. In stark contrast to the Scientific Management approach developed by Frederick W. Taylor [75] at the turn of the last century, where workers manipulated physical (tangible) materials and worked according to predefined processes and procedures, staff in international organizations handle mainly intangibles like information.

International organizations' knowledge workers' primary means of production, therefore, is not capital, land or labour, but rather the productive use of knowledge. Today, many international organizations have an increased need for more highly skilled knowledge workers. To illustrate this, a recent poll taken from the Chief Executive Board of the UN system (CEB) in 2004 [76], showed that there was a general increase in the professional staff ratio across all international organizations within the UN system. In 1994, the ratio of professional staff to general staff ranged from about 20% to 40%, whereas ten years later, in 2000, not a single organization had less than 30% professionals. Likewise, the work of general staff can be considered as knowledge work--important to the functioning and organizational memory of international organizations, because they are also expected to work effectively with ideas and knowledge [44, Article 101].

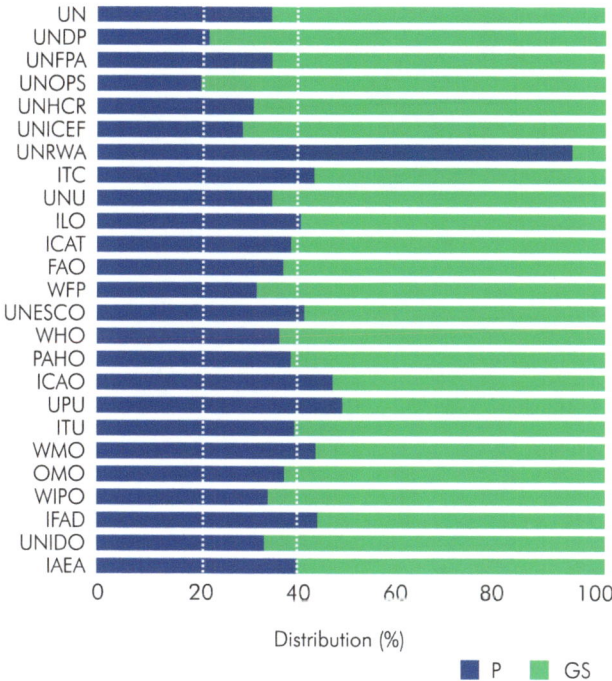

Figure 1.6 UN system general staff versus professional staff in 1994 (Source: [76])

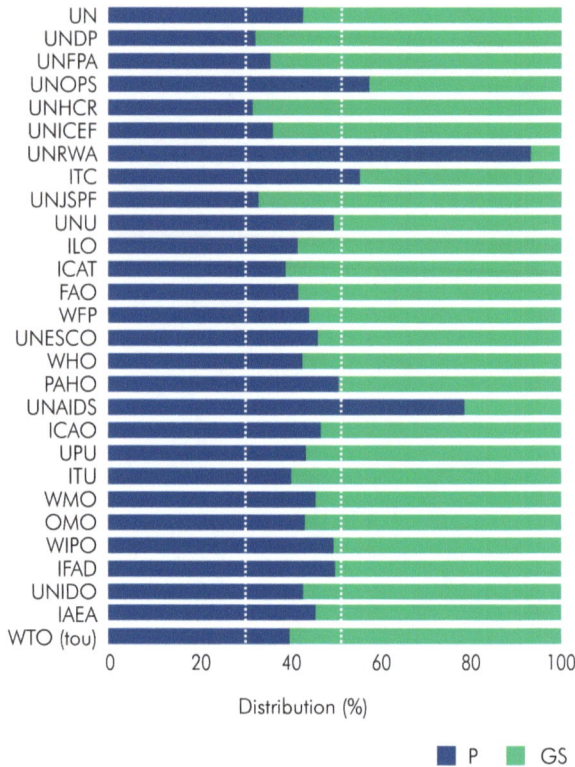

*Figure 1.7 UN system general staff versus professional staff
in 2004 (Source: [76])*

1.4.2   ORGANIZATIONAL CAPITAL

Organizational capital is systematized and packaged knowledge, plus
systems for leveraging a company's strengths and values to create
organizational capability [65]. This section highlights some resources
that can help enable an organization's capacity to add value to its
operations.

NON-DIGITAL TECHNOLOGY

In KM literature [74, 77], technology is generally taken to mean digital
media and networks. However it is also important to remember that
there are numerous other non-digital technologies that support

knowledge work. For example, paper is a significant and robust medium [78] that will not disappear any time soon. In fact, many international organizations are papyrocentric, relying on faxes and paper-based inter-office memos. Language also influences knowledge and meaning in international organizations. Many international organizations have more than one official language. For example, organizations within the United Nations (UN) system have six official languages (English, French, Spanish, Russian, Arabic and Chinese) and the EU manages over 23 languages.

DIGITAL TECHNOLOGY AND KNOWLEDGE MANAGEMENT SYSTEMS

Digital technology platforms and infrastructure are in constant flux, and new tools and technologies used for representing knowledge are being announced on a monthly basis. A short list of the current tools and software systems, known as knowledge management systems [79, 80], that can be used to support KM initiatives can be found below:

- **Public websites:** A place on the World Wide Web where an organization's public information is located.
- **Intranets:** private corporate websites that run on internet technologies.
- **Information retrieval programs:** Tools to search knowledge/data bases, as well as external knowledge sources to provide access to a wider variety of information.
- **Database management systems:** combine with intranets and information networks and can be used to provide a platform to build specific KM tools.
- **Document management (DM) systems:** provide the means for capturing, storing and distributing explicit knowledge representations in the form of documents.
- **Enterprise content management (ECM) systems:** These are technologies, tools and methods used to capture, manage, store, preserve, and deliver information, content and documents related to organizational processes [81].
- **Groupware:** Software that enables workgroups to communicate and collaborate.
- **Intelligent agents:** Software that can filter out useful information for a user.
- **Knowledge bases:** store knowledge of experts in the form of rules, cases and "best practices".

- **Expert databases:** store links to experts, their profiles, associated work and bibliographies.
- **Enterprise resource planning (ERP):** integrate (or attempt to integrate) all data and processes of an organization into a unified system. A typical ERP system will use multiple components of computer software and hardware to achieve the integration [82].

1.4.3   SOCIAL CAPITAL

Relational and social capital are intertwined [64], so this book shall use both terms interchangeably. In this section, a conceptual framework is provided for understanding social capital and related themes of cooperation and competition in international organizations.

SOCIAL CAPITAL

Since its introduction by Coleman [83], the concept of social capital has been cited in a wide range of social science literature and more recently in strategic management literature [84, 85]. These studies argue that social capital is a very important source of performance and competitive advantage. A common focus on people networks and trust, as well as value derived from networking in general, is implied (cf. Table 1.2).

Table 1.2: Definitions of social capital

Nahapiet [62]	Bourdieu [86]	Putnam [87]
… the actual and potential resources embedded within, available through, and derived from the network of relationships processed by an individual or social unit. Social capital thus comprises both network and assets that may be mobilized through that network	… the sum of the resources, actual or virtual, that accrue to an individual or group by virtue or possessing a durable network of more or less institutionalized relationships of mutual acquaintance and recognition	… features of social organizations such as networks, norms, and social trust that facilitate coordination and cooperation for mutual benefit

Unlike human capital (in people's heads) and organizational capital (owned by the organization), social capital is found in the nature of relationships, both formal and informal and, like human capital, is not owned by the organization. Although much literature talks about the positive effects of social capital, it can also have negative effects on organizational performance. For example, competition among funds and programs in many international organizations' technical assistance programs are accentuated and sometimes rendered ineffective by globalization of political, economic and cultural processes [88]. Most international organizations raise a large portion of their technical cooperation funds directly from donors, leading to competition among them for resources.

COLLABORATION AND COMPETITION

Competitive advantage, which can be gained through the application of KM practice, is underscored by both industry practitioners and academics alike [6, 55, 61, 89]. However, the idea of competition has been challenged by business studies academics like Adam Brandenburger of the Harvard Business School and Barry Nalebuff of the Yale School of Management [90]. They argue, using game theory [91], that organizations can gain advantage by means of a judicious mixture of competition and cooperation—through what they termed as "coopetition".

After numerous public protests at WTO meetings [92], following the Millennium Development Goals [88] signed by world leaders in 2000, there is a renewed appreciation that globalization does not have to further accentuate the divisions of the world into rich and poor[93]. If international issues, including issues related to security, the environment, technical assistance and poverty reduction are to be better addressed by international organizations, what is needed is a more "coopetitive" approach--an approach where stakeholders collaborate for the greater good of the international community—in spite of short term gains of not cooperating.

1.5   SUMMARY

A review of literature relating to KM led to the identification of several unique features of international organizations. International organizations comprise of its member countries and they perform normative and operational functions. An international organization can be classified according to its functional orientation, depending on the nature of its mandate and the bulk of its activities. International organizations do not exist for profits or market share, but have a significant purpose of trust—made explicit in their mandate. They function to benefit a variety of stakeholders. The intellectual capital of international organizations, including their human, organization and social capital components, represents unique intangible components that are frequently cited as having a critical impact on KM

These are:

- **Human capital:** the competence, intellectual agility and attitudes of employees—knowledge—that are used in the value creation process [65]. These resources are, by definition, not owned by the organization and if nurtured can create increasing returns [66, 67]. Human capital includes intangible dimensions of knowledge (tacit/explicit) and the process of externalization and integration of knowledge.
- **Organizational capital:** systematized and packaged knowledge, plus systems for leveraging a company's innovative strength and value creating organizational capability [65]. Organizational resources that can help enable an organization's capacity to add value to its operations include non-digital technology, as well as digital technology.
- **Social capital:** While there are many definitions of this term, a common focus on networks and trust, as well as value derived from networking in general, is implied in the term (cf. Table 1.2). Although much literature talks about the positive effects of social capital, it can also have negative effects on organizational performance and opportunism with regards to competition. In the context of international organizations' operational functions (cf. section 1.2), competition for resources to fund programs is at issue and, regarding normative functions (cf. Section 1.2), the need for collaboration and cooperation among stakeholders, with political agendas, are vital to reach common consensus.

1.6 CONCLUSION

These areas from literature summarize what are critical factors for managing knowledge in organizations. They each represent aspects of an international organization and its intellectual capital that a knowledge manager needs to be aware of, either with a view to taking specific actions to address them, or at least be aware of the impact they have on the organization. However, given that research into KM in organizations does not take into account the idiosyncratic context of international organizations, including their functions and related issues of global governance, politics, collaboration and diplomacy in both impersonal and interpersonal relations among countries, raises serious questions of whether current research in KM adequately addresses the functioning of international organizations. These larger issues have informed this research, and are addressed in the following chapters.

CHAPTER 2
CASE STUDIES

Progression to becoming more knowledge focused in the international organizations studied has not been linear; in fact all organizations are still learning how to do it. This section describes the context in each organization, detailing their unique storylines. All storylines reflects on the analysis in the selective coding phase of research [94]. Furthermore, selective coding, the relationships between the categories, established during open and axial coding phases (cf. Appendix B)[94], is illustrated within each storyline (cf. Figure 2.1, Figure 2.5, Figure 2.7, Figure 2.9, Figure 2.11, Figure 2.12, Figure 2.17 and Figure 2.19). Selective coding enabled the integration of categories into a core category "becoming knowledge focused", and was found to meet the characteristics of the basic social process (BSP) in organizations [94, 95].

The bold text in the illustrations of selective coding (cf. Figure 2.1, Figure 2.5, Figure 2.7, Figure 2.9, Figure 2.11, Figure 2.12, Figure 2.17 and Figure 2.19) depicts the main drivers for becoming knowledge focused, as well as the main outcome of becoming knowledge focused—increased "awareness" (see Appendix A for definitions of concepts).

2.1 IAEA STORYLINE

The International Atomic energy Agency (IAEA) serves as the world's central intergovernmental forum in the area of peaceful nuclear technology applications, transfer and safeguards.

In becoming knowledge focused, progression was from an initial critical phase, often described by management as "skills [nuclear scientists and engineers] are drying up", to an awareness of the challenges of managing knowledge expressed as "we have to get better at KM". For example, the Director General of the IAEA, Mohamed Elbaradei, in his statement to the 47th regular session of the IAEA General Conference in 2003, said:

> *...whether or not nuclear power witnesses an expansion in the coming decades, it is essential that we preserve nuclear scientific and technical competence for safe operations of existing facilities and applications. Effective management of nuclear knowledge should include succession planning for the nuclear work force, the maintenance of the "nuclear safety case" for operational reactors and retention of the nuclear knowledge accumulated over the past six decades*

EXTERNAL KNOWLEDGE MANAGEMENT CHALLENGES

In the IAEA, the external context revolved around the attrition of technical nuclear competence in the industry, exacerbated by, (a) government deregulation of the energy markets, (b) safety of operating, upgrading or decommissioning and decontaminating aging facilities, (c) negative public perceptions of the nuclear energy, shaped in part by well-known nuclear image issues—the memory of the Hiroshima and Nagasaki bombings; Calder Hall, Three Mile Island and Chernobyl nuclear plant disasters; and waste management problems, (d) global security concerns, including terrorism and nuclear proliferation and the need for changes to processes/procedures and technologies to keep up with demand for more accurate inspections and verifications and, (e) changes in geopolitical climate after the Cold War, including the rise of global energy security and environmental concerns—areas where nuclear energy can become increasingly useful. The external forces meant that the apparent skills' loss would affect the industry and by extension the IAEA's ability to carry out its mandate [96]: "to accelerate the contribution of nuclear energy for peaceful purposes".

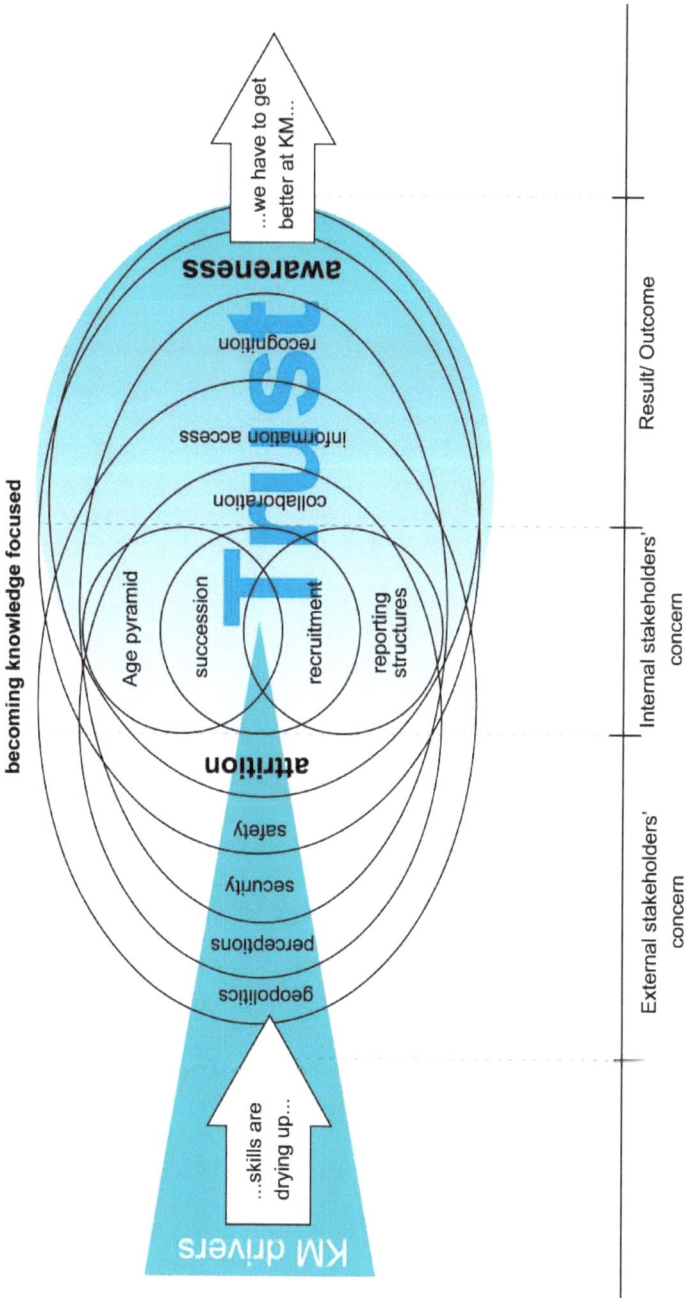

Figure 2.1: Relationship of categories and core category for the IAEA

INTERNAL KNOWLEDGE MANAGEMENT CHALLENGES

The internal context of the IAEA revolved around an awareness of the need for KM. For example, the skills' scarcity in the nuclear industry was affecting recruitment in nuclear sciences posts in the agency that made up to 70% of the professional workforce—"...sometimes those scarce specialists cannot be released by their governments". Some managers admitted that the attrition rate in the industry could have "catastrophic" effects on the organization because of "old-timers" who will be leaving the agency over the next 5 years, causing what some managers called an "age pyramid".

The recruitment challenges were further exacerbated by the statutory requirements made in 1956 [96], where member countries stated that the number of permanent staff "remain at a minimum" [96]. Consequently, 60% of the staff stay no longer than 7 years (some contracts are for as little as 6 months). This means that the organization is constantly "bringing people in and processing them out". The recruitment challenges and statutory turnover requirements of the Agency often led to gaps in projects, resulting in "handover that is not well passed on". For example, "a new staff member may find a manuscript that has not been finished, and is not in his particular area of competence, but needs to take action on it...it is then passed on to the publications section [which] may not be aware of it...".

KM was then seen as a tool for addressing these challenges at the micro level—particularly the issue of succession planning for internal stakeholders and at the macro level, a level beyond the organization, including the "preservation of nuclear knowledge" in the industry.

KNOWLEDGE MANAGEMENT INTERVENTIONS

The organization tackled the issue of managing knowledge by focusing on enhancing its intellectual capital assets(cf. Section 1.4), those intangibles that drive value for the organization (cf. Figure 1.3)—from the perspectives of the internal and external stakeholders.

The organizational capital, specifically the Agency's International Nuclear Information System (INIS), a bespoke portal system, developed to allow access to the IAEA's database, was put on the Internet, overcoming hurdles of distance by increasing access and encouraging contributions from specialists in the field.

More than 250,000 electronic full-text documents were added in 2004, and it had by then gained over 1 million authorized users. Students and academics at over 270 universities were also given free access to the portal.

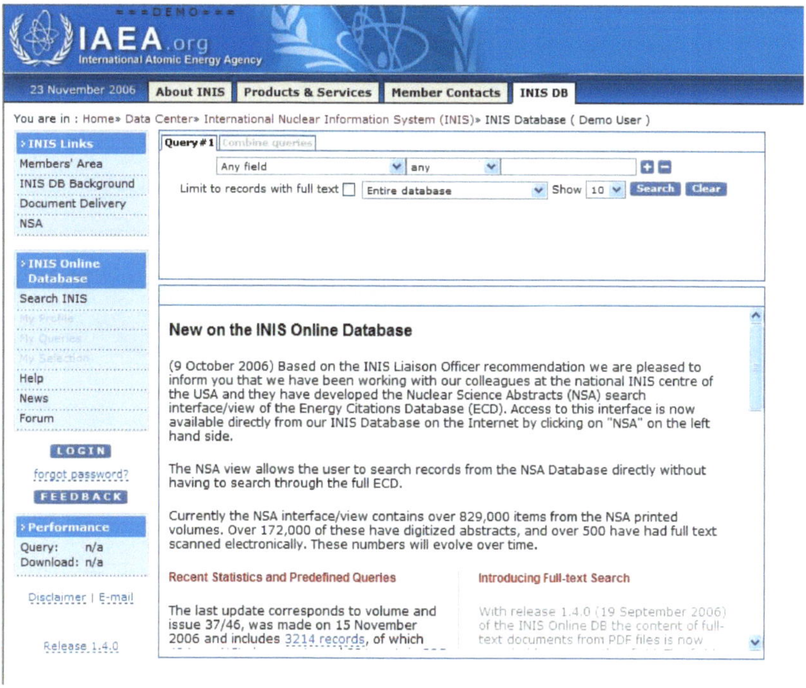

Figure 2.2: The INIS portal (demo version)

The INIS portal, also referred to as the knowledge portal, used both the personalization and codification strategies [5]; that is, the knowledge portal is used for linking people to documents, as well as to link people together. The INIS database contains over 2.7 million "codified" bibliographic records and full text documents. By searching recent entries, one can find experts who are presently active in a given domain, who can help direct enquires to databases and systems to find more detailed information. In addition, there is an IAEA Knowledge Desk (Figure 2.4) where one can contact the Agency directly for queries related to nuclear science.

Economic, Environmental,
Legal and Safeguards
8%

Life Sciences
17%

Atomic, Molecular and
Condensed Matter Physics
10%

Fuel Cycle, Waste and
Radiochemistry
7%

Nuclear Power & Safety
13%

Nuclear Physics
11%

Nuclear Materials
9%

Engineering &
Instrumentation
9%

Elementary Particle
Physics
16%

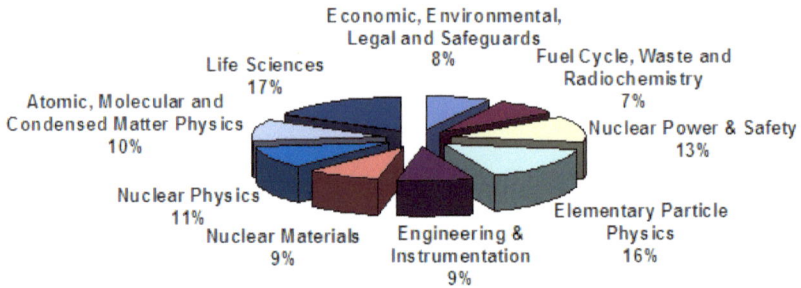

Figure 2.3: Scope of INIS database

IAEA.org
International Atomic Energy Agency

About IAEA | **R&D Focus** | Publications | Meetings | Jobs

You are in : IAEA.org » R&D Focus » Nuclear Knowledge Desk

> **R&D Focus**

Find-an-Expert Facility

**Nuclear Knowledge
Desk**

Nuclear Reactors
Knowledge Base

IAEA Web Resources

Internet Directory

Energy & Env. Data
Reference Bank

World's Nuclear
Literature

Bibliometric Studies

> **IAEA Data Centre**

Statistics

Databases

Scientific Networks

Programme Sites

> **see also:**

INIS HOME

INIS Bibliographic
Database

IAEA Nuclear
Knowledge
Management HOME

Contact INIS

Nuclear Knowledge Desk

Ask-an-Expert facility

This facility is intended for students and professionals in nuclear and nuclear related fields. Users of the service who submit queries concerning nuclear R&D and applications will be put into contact with an expert on the relevant subject or will receive a reply from the Nuclear Knowledge Desk, as appropriate.

If you wish to use the facility, we ask you to:

- please give us your email address so that we can reply to you (we will not use it for any other purpose)
- please identify yourself, giving your name, affiliation and profession (every request is handled by a professional in the nuclear field who wants to know who he or she is talking to)
- please state the subject of your query in a concise phrase in the subject line of the email
- please state your query as precisely as possible, so that we can answer in the most efficient way

The Nuclear Knowledge Desk can be accessed via:

email: nkd@iaea.org
fax: +43 1 2600 29882
telephone: +43 1 2600 22790

Please note that if your query concerns:

- official business and program enquiries use: Official.Mail@iaea.org
- general information and press enquiries use: info@iaea.org
- IAEA Library Resources consult: http://www.iaea.org/DataCenter/Library/catresources.html
- issues of technical cooperation with the IAEA use: http://www-tc.iaea.org/tcweb/general/feedback/default.asp
- obtaining IAEA Publications use: sales.publications@iaea.org
- technical issues about the IAEA.org site use: Webmaster@iaea.org

Copyright 2003, International Atomic Energy Agency, P.O. Box 200, Wagramer Strasse 5, A-1400 Vienna, Austria
Telephone (+43) 1 2600-0; Facsimile (+43) 1 2600-7; E-mail: Official.Mail@iaea.org
Disclaimer

Figure 2.4: IAEA Knowledge Desk

The human capital in the industry was also strengthened by the Agency's capacity-building projects. The Agency founded–and continues to support–the World Nuclear University (WNU), together with the Nuclear Energy Agency (NEA) of the OECD, the World Association of Nuclear Operators (WANO), and the World Nuclear

Association (WNA). Although a virtual institution, the WNU mechanism of trans-national co-operation was formed to serve national governments seeking to strengthen their technological foundations for nuclear science and engineering. The WNU offers seasonal online and classroom-based courses to students and practitioners at participating educational institutions worldwide, co-ordinated from a central secretariat in London.

Another aspect of knowledge management dealt with recognizing the risks posed by safety at operational reactors. This is also known in the Agency as "maintaining the safety case". The Agency participates in the World Association of Nuclear Operators' workshops. These events allow plant managers to share their ideas on how best to capture undocumented tacit information of experienced workers.

The organization encourages collaboration in the industry, building its social capital. The Agency organized the first international seminar on nuclear knowledge management (NKM) in September 2004, inviting all stakeholders to participate, including academics, industry professionals and governments and relevant national/international organizations. The agency also hired a full time knowledge manager to head the INIS and nuclear knowledge management program, allocating manpower and human resources to the effort.

Specifically to address the internal knowledge management issue, a task force comprising a matrix of management staff from different departments formed a community of practice to try to further raise awareness among staff of the need to share knowledge and encourage managers to look into cross-cutting programs. The "Director General's briefs", a one page (A4) summary of regional developments in the nuclear field, is one example of a cross-cutting program, composed from evaluating travel reports of all staff stored in the database. The database uses an organizational taxonomy to simplify data entry, but the DG's briefs are "unstructured"—in the sense that they are simple Microsoft Word documents.

2.2 IMO STORYLINE

When the establishment of a specialized agency of the United Nations dealing with maritime affairs was first proposed, the main concern was to improve safety at sea [97]. Since 1948, when the organization was established, there has been a proliferation of committees and sub committees dealing with may facets of maritime safety. A few examples of IMO subcommittees are: The Safety of Navigation (NAV); Radiocommunications and Search and Rescue (COMSAR); Training and Watchkeeping (STW); Carriage of Dangerous Goods, Solid Cargoes and Containers (DSC); Ship Design and Equipment (DE); Fire Protection (FP); Stability and Load Lines and Fishing Vessel Safety (SLF); Flag State Implementation (FSI); and Bulk Liquids and Gases (BLG).

In order to meet the growing challenges of maritime safety through an increasing number of services, the IMO developed several disparate IT systems and adhoc services for managing its administrative (financial and managerial) and substantive activities. In becoming knowledge focused, therefore, there was a push both from management, member countries and IT to consolidate systems and to streamline the primary activities of the organization. IMO sought consultation from renowned management consultancies, such as MANNET, an international consultancy group, based in Geneva, Switzerland, that has worked with 25 other international organizations, and Deloitte and Touche.

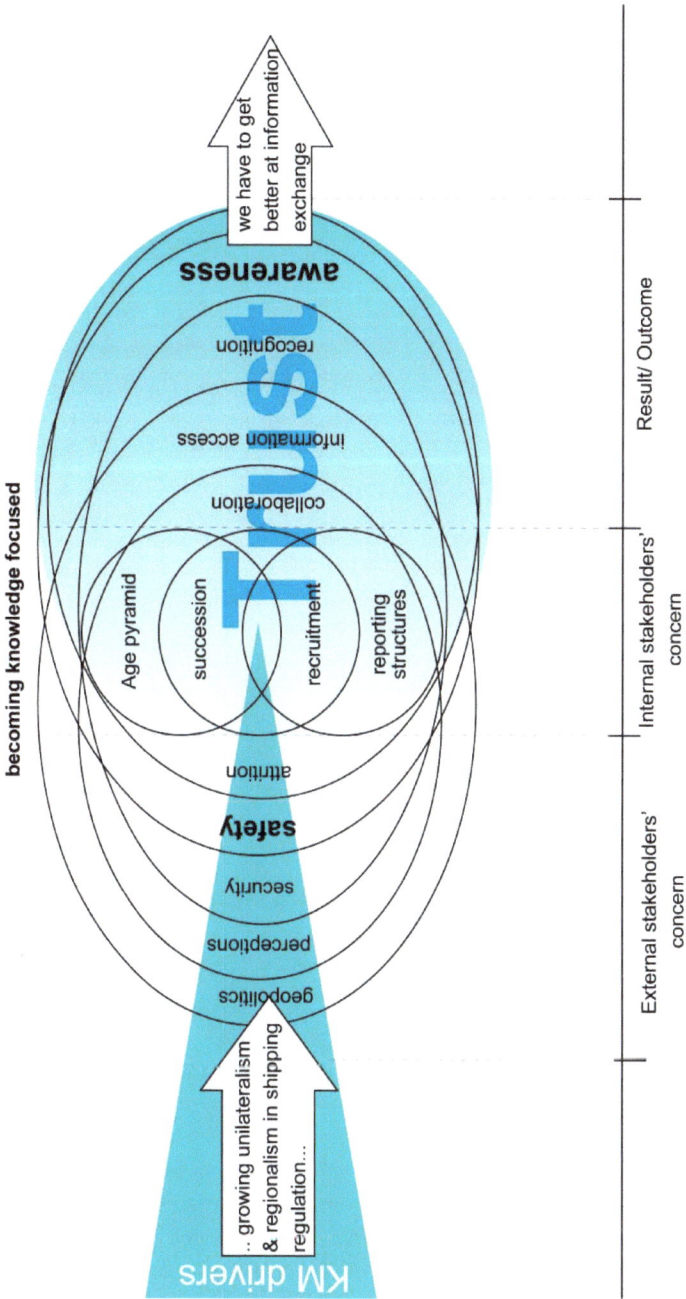

Figure 2.5: Relationship of categories and core category for the IMO

EXTERNAL KNOWLEDGE MANAGEMENT CHALLENGES

In IMO, the external context revolved around enhancing the organizations authority, credibility and position as the world's pre-eminent maritime body [98] by addressing challenges to maritime environment, such as the negative perception of the shipping industry following several disasters, involving loss of life and environmental damage. For example, there was the Titanic disaster in 1912, the oil spills from Exxon Valdex in 1989, the Estonia sinking in 1994, the Erika sinking in 1999, as well as illegal waste disposal, such as discharge of ballasts, and water used for cleaning cargo tanks, and so on. Important IMO conventions like the safety of life at sea (SOLAS) and the international convention for the prevention of pollution from ships (MAROL) were amended as a result of these disasters. In spite of IMO's actions, some governments and other intergovernmental organizations felt that the amendments did not go far enough in addressing the issues. For example, following the Prestige disaster in 2002, the EU banned many single-hall ships from ports in Europe [99]. Thus how to preserve unity among its membership—against unilateralism and regionalism in the regulation of shipping – are the most important external challenge facing the organization [100].

INTERNAL KNOWLEDGE MANAGEMENT CHALLENGES

The increasing number of services and programs meant that the organization had an increased need for information exchange--particularly between the organization and its member countries. This was given the organic growth of its programs, based on external geopolitical concerns and perceptions related to shipping (see external KM challenged above), the IT systems and databases that had become inhomogeneous. IT and substantial units managed hundreds of disparate databases relating to ships and likewise technical cooperation expenditure and budgetary systems, including publication sales were largely papyrocentric and required a large number of staff to manage. Decisions required a lot of physical signatures from line managers and information from participating countries was not standardized. Sometimes information from member countries came in the mail, as paper based reports, while at other times they came through the email as excel spread sheets, and so on. The change management process was driven concurrently by member countries, members of management, and the IT department to address these inefficiencies.

KNOWLEDGE MANAGEMENT INTERVENTIONS IN IMO

Normatively, the organization continued to address its regulatory functions by managing conventions, providing a neutral trusted ground for negotiation and networking for member countries. Operationally, it provided technical assistance to countries, building capacity to meet the international standards in shipping. For example, the global programme on maritime port security is a technical assistance response to developing countries' needs to upgrade infrastructure and training to meet several regulatory standards.

In order to improve human capital in the maritime industry, the organization and its member countries established several educational institutions, such as (a) the World Maritime University in Sweden [101], (b) the International Maritime Law institute in Malta [102], which forms part of the University of Malta, and (c) The international Maritime Academy, in Italy. All institutions provide courses and training leading to internationally recognized certificates and degrees --from bachelor's to doctorate level.

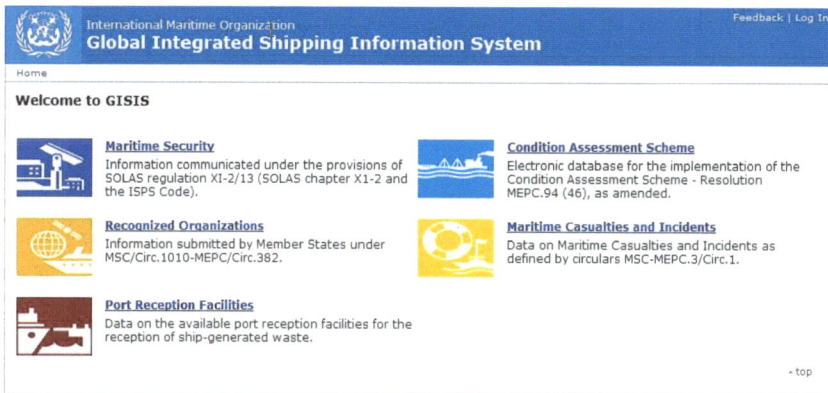

Figure 2.6: GISIS portal used to consolidate all information related to shipping

Internally, the organization embarked on a change management program. The program addressed administrative issues by implementing Enterprise Resource Management (ERP) systems. The ERP systems addressed issues related to administration and budgeting. The Global Integrated Shipping Information System (GISIS) was also architected and implemented to consolidate all disparate systems relating to shipping information. The system allowed for a single point of contact with the organization for sharing information. Member country users (port officials, government agencies and national and international regulatory bodies) were mandated to participate in sharing information via the GISIS system. As a result, several posts were abolished and remaining staff had to be retrained to take advantage of the new systems implemented as part of the change management program.

2.3 OFID STORYLINE

The OPEC Fund for International Development (OFID) is an international development finance institution (IFI), established by the member countries of OPEC in 1976. Shortly after its formation, it was under pressure to deliver value to developing countries, and was mandated to exclude OPEC member countries themselves. In order to meet its obligations expeditiously, it recruited only very experienced staff from other IFIs like the World Bank and the International Monetary Fund, and so on. This created an age pyramid in the mid to late 1990s, where after two decades, a significant proportion (over 30%) of its experienced staff were nearing their retirement. At the same time, when the organization was facing the age pyramid, it expanded its activities to include the private sector in 1998, in addition its public sector funding and programs. The private sector lending was created in response to growing emphasis on private enterprise by beneficiary countries, as well as the increasing need among private enterprises for medium and long-term financial support.

EXTERNAL KNOWLEDGE MANAGEMENT CHALLENGES

Crippling external debt burden has been increasingly acknowledged as a major constraint on the ability of the world's poorest countries to pursue sustainable development and alleviate poverty [103]. Against this background, International Finance Institutions (IFIs), including the Bretton Woods institutions and 180 governments around the world endorsed several programs aimed at helping alleviate poverty. For example, programs like the Heavily Indebted Poor Countries (HIPC) initiative in September 1996; the Millennium Development Goals in 2000 [45]; and more recently the Multilateral Debt Relief Initiative (MDRI) in 2006 have been endorsed by all members countries of major IFIs. For OFID's part, supporting these growing number of initiatives means strategically collaborating with other similar institutions to provide a catalytic effect and to avoid duplication and wasted resources [104].

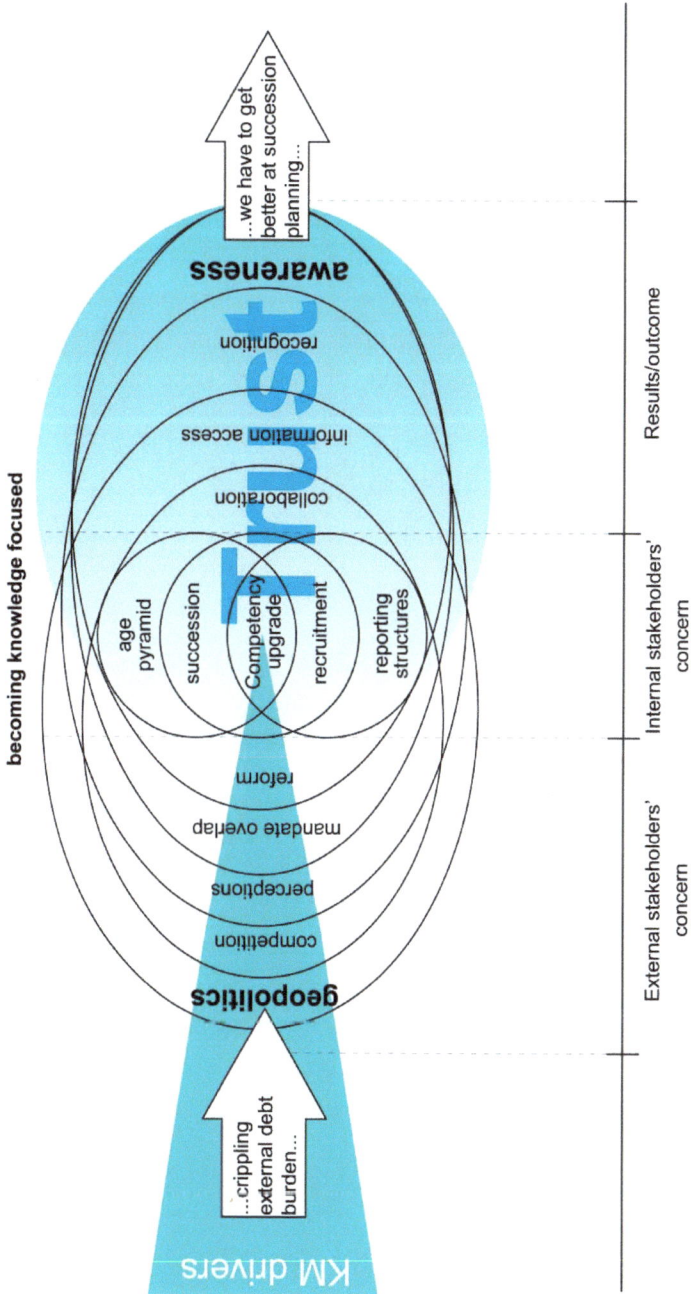

Figure 2.7: Relationship of categories and core category for OFID

INTERNAL KNOWLEDGE MANAGEMENT CHALLENGES

Internally, the organization's management was focused on upgrading the competencies of the organization, in order to face the growing challenges of its expanding activities. The organization opened the private sector operations in response to demands in recipient countries during the periods when experienced staff were retiring in the 1990s. This meant that the organization risked loosing much of its institutional memory (the tacit and explicit knowledge) with the departure of its seasoned staff. Document and records management, particularly in the form of emails, were not centrally stored and managed, so these compounded the issues of managing knowledge.

KNOWLEDGE MANAGEMENT INTERVENTIONS

The organization conducted manpower planning to determine exactly how many key staff will be retiring. It also hired a mix of highly experienced (15 years and above) staff as managers in the newly formed private sector section, as well as and some junior staff as assistants. Many junior staff members were hired from college that were trained and mentored along side the more experienced staff. A documents' management system was purchased and implemented to automate the document and records retention policy. An ERP system was implemented to assist in human resources management, budgets and accounting. The systems deployed were intended to demystify work processes and to streamline the management of records and operations of the organization. A corporate identity was created to strengthen the organization's image, as a credible institution with readily discernable goals and objectives. This corporate identity was applied to all visual communications channels, including the website, intranet (cf. Figure 2.8), publications and the extranet.

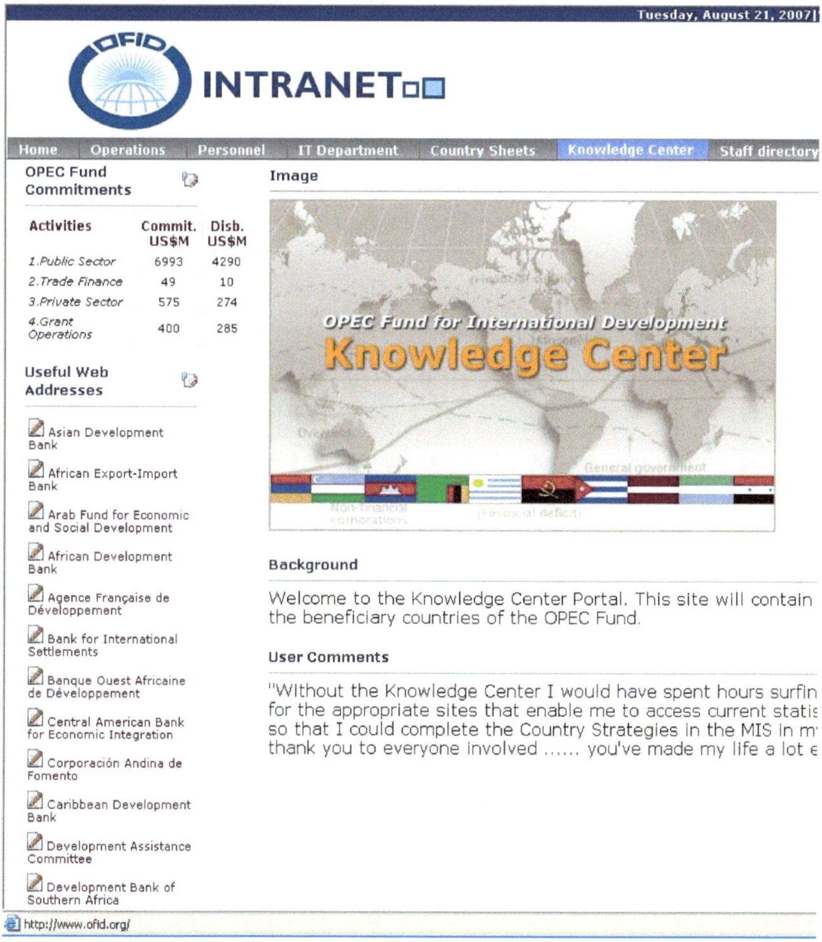

Figure 2.8: OPEC fund intranet

2.4 OPEC STORYLINE

OPEC is focused on stabilizing the international oil market, in order to ensure that there is no harmful fluctuations, by unifying the policies of its member countries, regarding oil production.

Recent high oil prices have been generated by a complex combination of speculative worries and market fundamentals[105]. It is against this background that consuming countries all over the world have expressed increasing concern over the secure flow of oil and reasonable and stable prices. They have introduced various policies [106, 107], and are beginning to subsidize competing fuels, and increasing taxes on oil [108]. OPEC countries have equally expressed concern for predictable demand for oil at adequate prices for their exhaustible resources [32].

In order to meet the organization's mandate [109] to secure "an efficient, economic and regular supply of oil to consuming nations" in the increasingly complex oil markets, the organization has focused on increasing its relations and trust between producers and consumers of oil [110]:

> *Over the past 15 years, OPEC has been actively involved in the establishment and development of the foremost producer/consumer dialogue at the political level, the International Energy Forum (IEF)...It [OPEC] also helped set up the Joint Oil Data Initiative ...with five intergovernmental organizations,...whose focus is on advancing the transparency, quality and timeliness and flows of energy market data...OPEC recently expanded and enhanced dialogue with...the EU, China, Russia, Japan and the International Energy Agency (IEA)...*

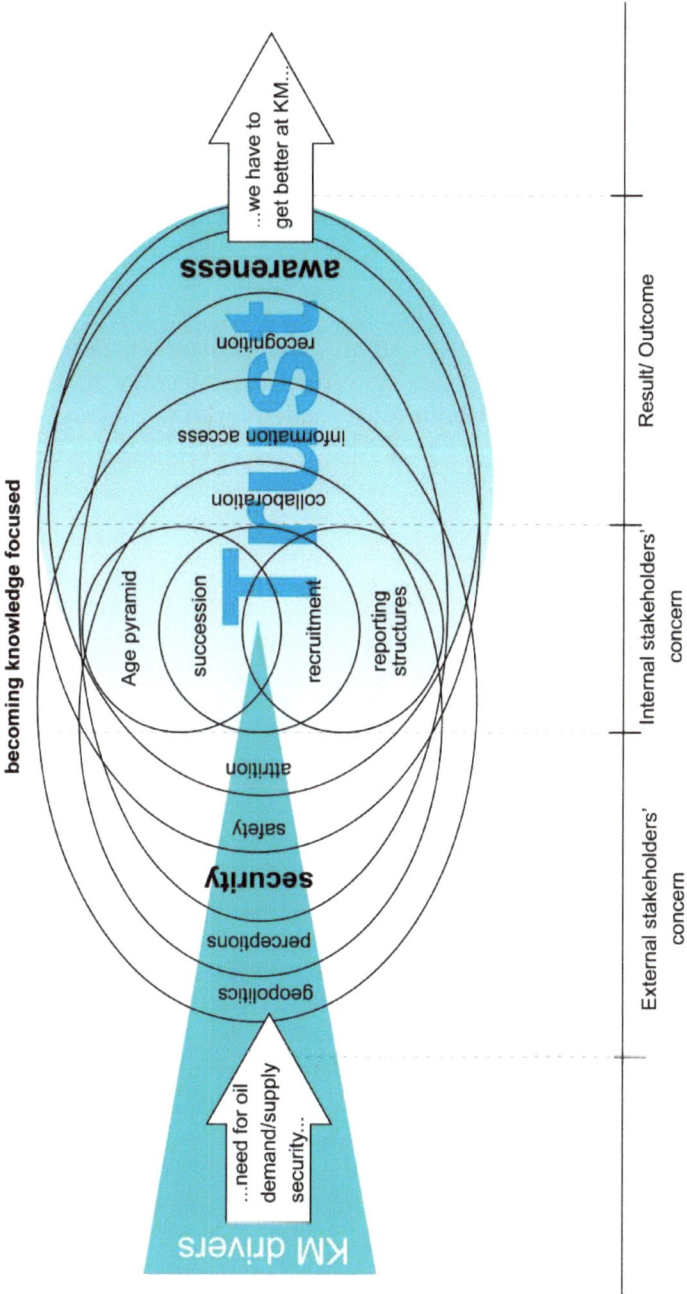

Figure 2.9: Relationship of categories and core category for OPEC

EXTERNAL KNOWLEDGE MANAGEMENT CHALLENGES

In OPEC, the external context revolved around oil supply/demand security issues, affected by geopolitics, such as, (a) government deregulation of the energy markets, (b) lack of governments (particularly in the US and EU) investments in downstream refinery capacity, (c) the importance of the environment and sustainable development issues, (d) governments policies towards oil, including high levels of taxation—(combined taxation levels in the G7 countries alone exceeds the total revenue of eleven OPEC member countries, by over 200 billion US dollars [108]), (e) negative public perception of the oil industry, (f) decreasing academic interest in the oil industry, affecting the skilled labour force needed for upstream and downstream activities (g) the rising cost of fuel for transportation and (h) fears of the limits of growth [25].

INTERNAL KNOWLEDGE MANAGEMENT CHALLENGES

The internal challenges of the organization focused on how to leverage the intellectual capital of the OPEC Secretariat and its staff to meet the external challenges.

The organization has a three-tiered staffing structure. The first level consists of supervisory and managerial positions reserved for member country nationals. The second level consists of professionals that can be recruited internationally, and finally there are the general staff. Over 30% of those recruited at level 2 will be reaching the age of retirement in the next decade.

The growing complexity in the oil market means that member countries need more timely bespoke reports and research covering more interdisciplinary subjects, including topics related to the environment, world trade, geopolitics, and strategy scenarios, and so on [32]. The organization faces difficulties in filling specialist vacancies for staff at level 1, as a result of waning academic interest in the oil industry in some member countries. The recruitment challenge was further exacerbated by the statutory turnover of 5 years for officer positions.

Finally, the organization is very papyrocentric. Interdepartmental memos, are handwritten to be official. Electronic email was often used by some staff as their private knowledge base. The documents that were stored and backed up on shared network drives were not systematically managed. Organization memory of documents was often lost with PC hardware upgrades.

KNOWLEDGE MANAGEMENT INTERVENTIONS

OPEC tackled the challenges mentioned above by focusing on ways to strengthen the intellectual capital of the organization. At the human capital level, the organization focused more on using cross cutting projects in the Research Departments to meet the growing demands of the member counties for bespoke reports in the oil market. For example, for oil market projections the Petroleum Market Analysis Department (PMAD) depends on the Data Services Department (DSD), and for longer term projections PMAD requires input from the Energy Studies Department (ESD). Numerous small groups of professionals were formed into task forces to study particular facets of the oil industry. As part this initiative to improve collaboration and productivity of networks, the organization started formally training its entire staff on "soft skills", like presentation skills and communication skills, delivered by Learning Tree®, a management training institute.

Several new positions were also created to address manpower shortages in meeting the needs of the organization. For example, the environmental analyst and legal advisor on international affairs positions were created and filled. Strategically, more professional positions are anticipated in the near future, following plans to build a new eight-storey building (at Wipplingerstrasse 33) in 2008 that is almost three times as large as the current premises.

In order to strengthen the organizational capital, several new IT systems were implemented. The portal system was designed and implemented to allow information and applications to be disseminated to both the staff and member countries with appropriate security. (Member countries users are referred to as "intranet users", even though they are not part of the organizations staff). An information survey was conducted and a retention policy was created to ensure that important organizational transactions and activities are properly managed. An electronic records management (ERM) system has been proposed (but not yet implemented).

In order to make more sense of data held by the organization, an integrated oil market information system, also known as a "chart bank", is being developed and piloted in-house. The system consolidates various databases about the oil market held in the

Secretariat and produces many complex interrelated charts that can be quarried, in order to simplify and quicken the analysis process.

With regards to the relational capital of the organization, several international formal and informal dialogues and workshops have been institutionalized. The Joint Data Oil Initiative (JODI) the International Energy Forum (IEF), and the EU-OPEC Energy Dialogue, and so on, [111] are now regularly held.

The organization's website uses Web 2.0 concepts [112], and technologies, but in a controlled way. It publishes regular podcasts, RSS feeds, email alerts, as well as live and on-demand video, around a community of experts in the oil industry. A media reporter in the industry is seconded to conduct interviews with OPEC management, Member country officials and experts in the oil industry during major OPEC events. The interviews are published (unedited) live and later (edited) on-demand on the website to supplement the opening address and the press conference during the OPEC conferences for example (cf. Figure 2.10).

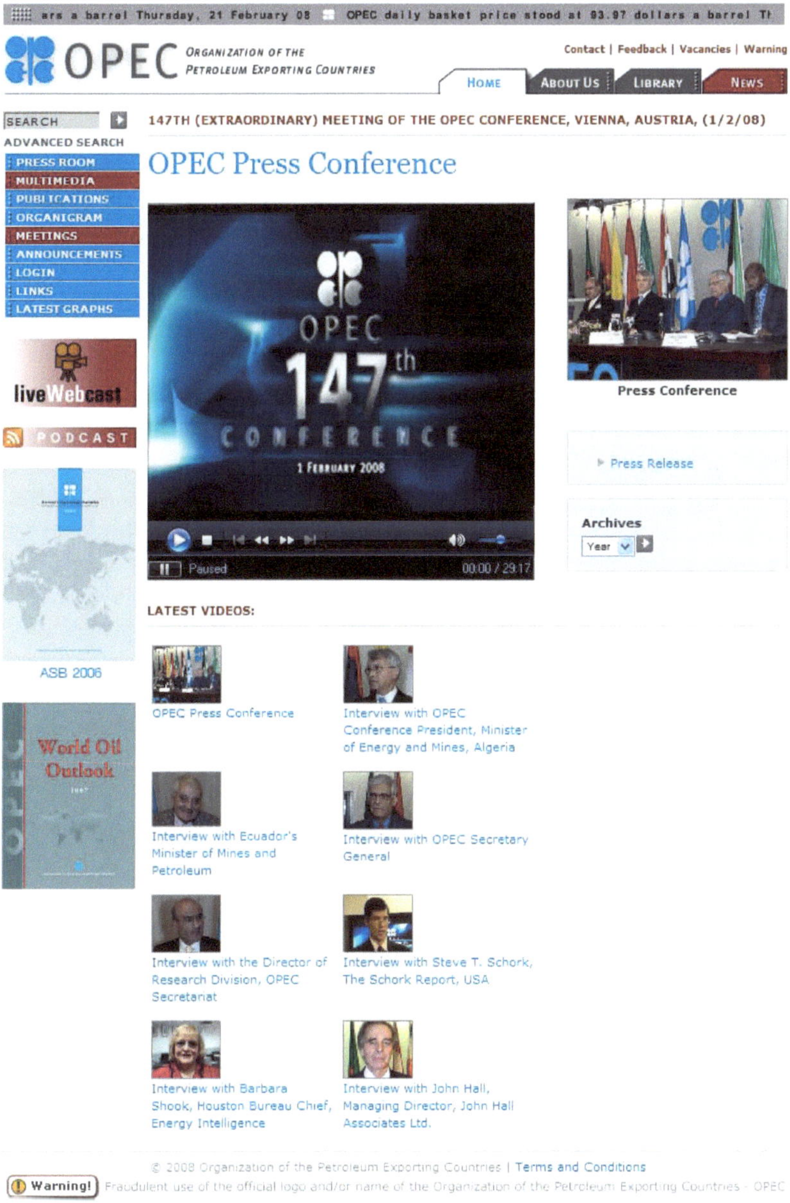

Figure 2.10: OPEC website

2.5 OSCE STORYLINE

OSCE is an organization that allocates about 85% of its resources to field operations. It works in the Balkans, Eastern Europe, the Caucasus and increasingly in Central Asia. Its field operations cover a wide range of activities, such as support to local elections, the creation of ombudsmen offices, confidence-building measures, the training of multi-ethnic policing and border monitoring.

In becoming knowledge focused, progression was from an initial critical phase of very rapid expansion—by over 2,000% in the first 10 years. From an IT perspective, this rapid expansion resulted in "a very inhomogeneous environment,…with decentralized systems,…various hardware and software platforms,… and a menagerie of communication avenues…" The challenge of KM was further exacerbated by the statutory turnover, a human resources policy where all professional staff were contractually limited to work in the organization, ranging from a few weeks to a maximum of 7years. This situation meant that organizational memory was lost when staff members leave. A climax of dissatisfaction among member countries was reached in 2000 when the Governing body of the OSCE put a freeze on all IT development, on the condition that an OSCE-wide IT strategy be developed and implemented.

EXTERNAL KM CHALLENGES

The key external challenge facing the organization today is making sure that it continues to add value in countries where it operates. During the 1990s, intra- and inter-state conflicts were the number one priority of the OSCE and, during this period, operations grew very rapidly. It developed unmatched competencies in conflict prevention, crisis management and post-conflict rehabilitation. Today, those competences have overlapped with larger organizations like NATO and the EU. In the area of security, its competences now overlap with the competences of NATO, while in the area of democracy-building and human rights its competencies overlap with those of the EU [113]. Moreover, the Russian Federation and Western regions (EU and the USA) disagree on how to reform the organization's programs, based on national/regional interests [113]. These disagreements are, in part, fuelled by the growing influence of the West in post-Soviet spaces.

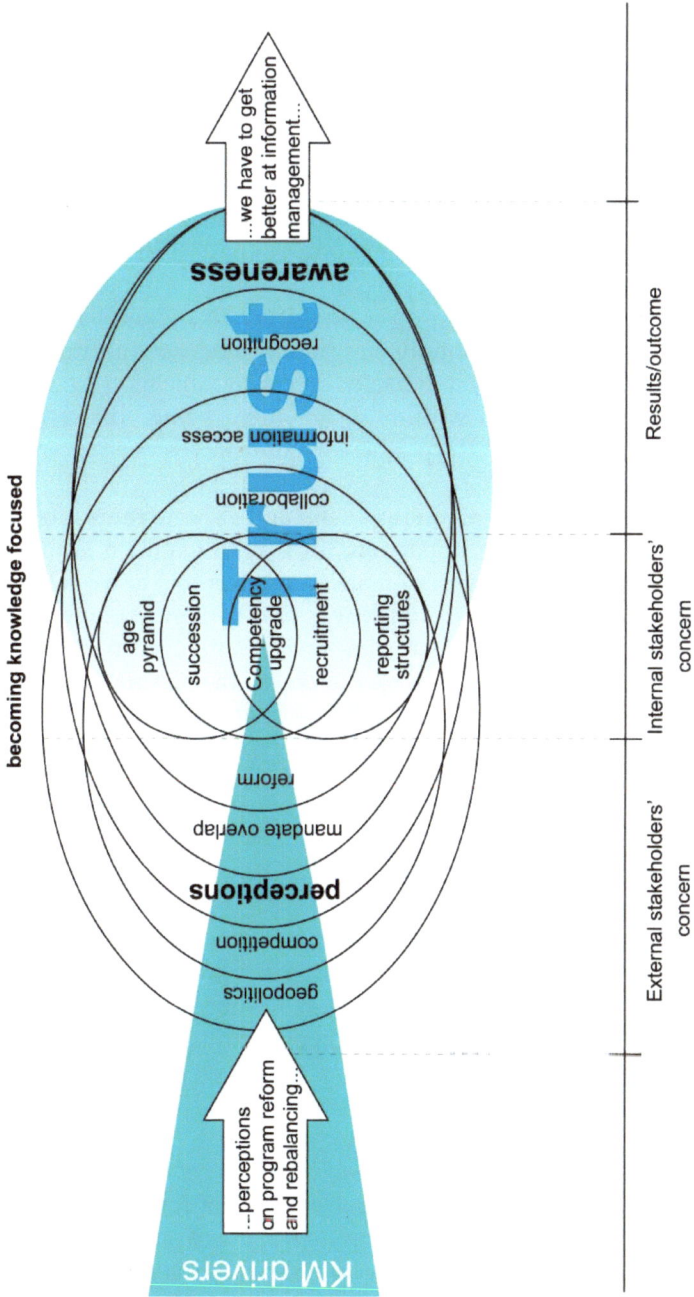

Figure 2.11: Relationship of categories and core category for OSCE

INTERNAL KM CHALLENGES

The OSCE is often called upon to react swiftly to new political developments and to accomplish tasks at short notice. Hence, the legal, logistical and technical (network) requirements for operating in post-war areas meant that IT was central to efficiency and effective operations. For example, tasks such as the organization of municipal elections in Kosovo, implementing border controls in the Caucasus and establishing multiethnic policing in the former Yugoslav republic of Macedonia required setting up makeshift offices with IT infrastructure for staff. "All these operations are time bound…owing much of their success to the ability and capacity of the organization to launch and dismantle operations within days after being directed by its policymaking body…", the permanent council.

There often was little planning available to the organization to meet political mandates. The impact on HR was to maintain a pool of very experienced international staff that can be recruited to work for various periods at a time. The drawback was that project documentation and lessons learned were lost due to the high staff turnover. The knowledge loss was further exacerbated by an inhomogeneous IT environment at various field offices. Eventually, diplomats in the governing bodies of the organization expressed their dissatisfaction with the status quo by freezing IT financial resources in 2000, pending the adoption of an OSCE-wide IT strategy.

KM INTERVENTIONS AT OSCE

Core to the management agenda, a comprehensive strategy for reforming resource management of the OSCE, introduced by the Secretary General, was the Integrated Resource Management System (IRMA) and dedicated portable client workstations, called "yellow laptop". When the governing body approved the resources for the system, they described the IRMA as follows [114]:

> …*IRMA is the operational implementation of the Management Agenda program agreed at Bucharest in 2001. It is a program that will ensure that the OSCE develops and implements a continually improving model of best practice in management and administration. It will create for the OSCE a professional, cost efficient, budget-based management structure that will ensure that our future operational activities are conducted in the most effective and transparent manner…*

Other facets of information and knowledge management still being implemented include the common web-based portal system with security rights; a common document and records management system; and a common retention policy [115].

2.6 UNIDO STORYLINE

In becoming knowledge-focused, progression was from an initial critical phase, where external stakeholders demanded "improved program delivery" [116] that addressed individual member countries' evolving developmental needs, and donor support requirements, driven in part by changes in the geopolitical climate. This led the organization to focus on managing various aspects of its intellectual capital, including its human, relational and organizational capital. Addressing external and internal stakeholder concerns led the organization to a greater awareness of the challenges of knowledge management.

EXTERNAL KM CHALLENGES

In UNIDO, the external context revolved around growing pressure from the international community for better methods to define the needs, interests and priorities in the organization's technical co-operation programs. However, these requirements were heavily influenced by politics.

The Cold War gave increasing scope for operational activities in support of development, as the protagonists were motivated by a desire to secure political influence in the developing world [13]. The increasing number of UN funds and programs, such as UNDP, WFP, UNFPA, UNICEF and UNHCR, in addition to those of UNIDO, expanded their institutional co-operation machinery worldwide without any clear programmatic focus, resulting in program overlap. For example, UNIDO, working in such areas as the environment, trade and agriculture, sometimes overlapped with the technical assistance operations of UNEP, UNCTAD and the FAO.

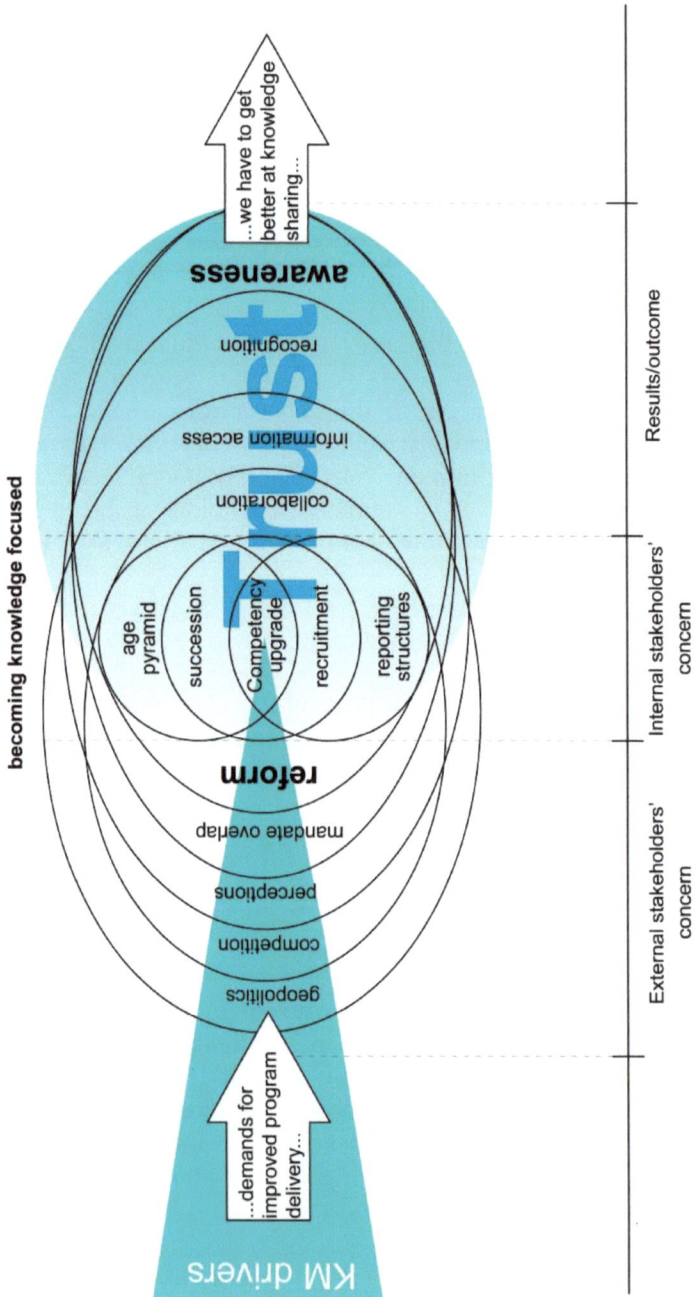

Figure 2.12: Relationship of categories and core category for UNIDO

Programmatic reforms in the operational activities of UNIDO were driven mainly by, (1) the end of the Cold War, with the reduction or cessation of donor support from the Former Soviet Union, and fewer political incentives from the West, (2) economic globalization, (3) liberalization of international and domestic trading environments and (4) the knowledge-based economy, which introduced numerous competitive pressures that many developing countries are ill-equipped to meet. These factors meant that the organization had to focus its program delivery to meet increasing pressure from donor countries, on the one hand, and recipient countries, on the other, for better quality strategies for industrial development. Likewise, the recent international development objectives, as stated in the Millennium Development Goals (MDG) in 2000 [88], provided added impetus for focusing the service knowledge activities of the organization.

INTERNAL KM CHALLENGES

Programmatic reform implemented in UNIDO led to further challenges for the organization as it managed its own human resources and internal dynamics. Like the IAEA, UNIDO also experienced a skill shortage, but for a different reason. Due to the downsizing, a part of the reform process, the number of experienced professional staff was halved - from 1,400 to 700, leaving a skeleton staff of only the most experienced people to meet its business plan—70% of whom hold PhDs, and have established considerable skills and experience, distinct methods of approach, and professional contacts. The new business plan called for a reduction in the number of programs undertaken by the organization—in 1997 there were about 250 different programs, which by 2002 had been reduced to just eight integrated programs. This meant that a greater number of staff had to learn to work in teams to share knowledge.

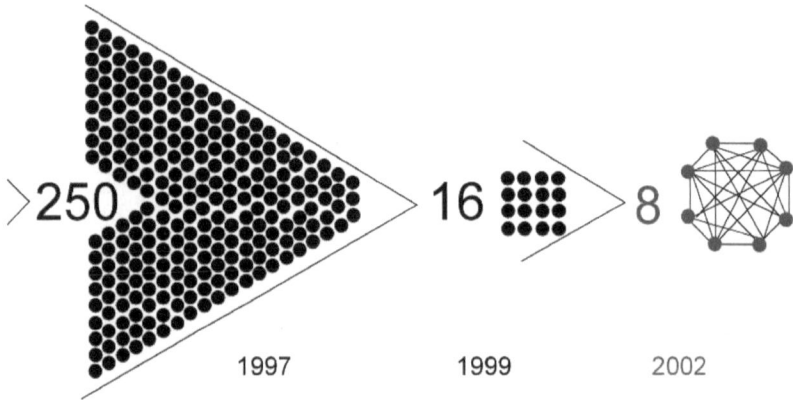

Figure 2.13: UNIDO program reform (adapted from: [14])

KM INTERVENTIONS IN UNIDO

The implications of the business plan led to several drastic changes aimed at strengthening the organization's intellectual capital.

The human capital intervention focused on succession planning and competence-building of UNIDO staff. Recently, UNIDO realized that about 30% of its "superstars"—the highly specialised professionals implementing the business plan——will be reaching retirement age over the next 3 to 4 years. Unlike the IAEA, which has a statutory turnover, UNIDO relies upon the tacit knowledge and longevity of its experienced development practitioners. This meant that replacing them by planning for succession was given priority.

In the first nine months of Dr Kandeh Yumkella's term as UNIDO Director General, starting in January 2005, the organization conducted a skills' analysis to try to determine, (a) what skills the organization had, (b) what skills it might need in the future based on emerging trends in industrial development, (c) the levels of retirement and what this meant for institutional memory and, (d) how to bring in young professionals to bridge the gap. The Director General's focus on knowledge management included how to upgrade the human capital of the organization by "injecting new blood" into the system—so that once recruited, a number of junior professional staff could learn from the more experienced staff.

The organizational capital enhancement focused on changing the organizational culture, structure and improving information and communication technologies (ICT). Changing staff behaviour from "knowledge is power" or information hoarding—which was common prior to 1997—where there were more individual programs—to "knowledge-sharing" and teamwork where there are fewer but more integrated programs, meant that collaboration among stakeholders was a must. ICT tools developed for creating, storing and disseminating information—KMS tools (cf. Figure 3.6)—were implemented to ensure that all stakeholders remained abreast of developments and could collaborate across time zones and distances effectively.

For example, a knowledge portal called UNIDO Exchange was developed to provide a platform for the various actors in the public and private sectors, civil society and the policymaking community in general to enhance co-operation, establish dialogue and develop partnerships. The intranet, called the Infobase, was also developed to aid communication within the organization. The bureau for organisational learning and strategy was created in 2005. This new bureau was charged (among other responsibilities) with creating and disseminating research and lessons learned in field projects, using ICT, as well as linking those lessons learned back to strategic planning to improve the effectiveness of programs.

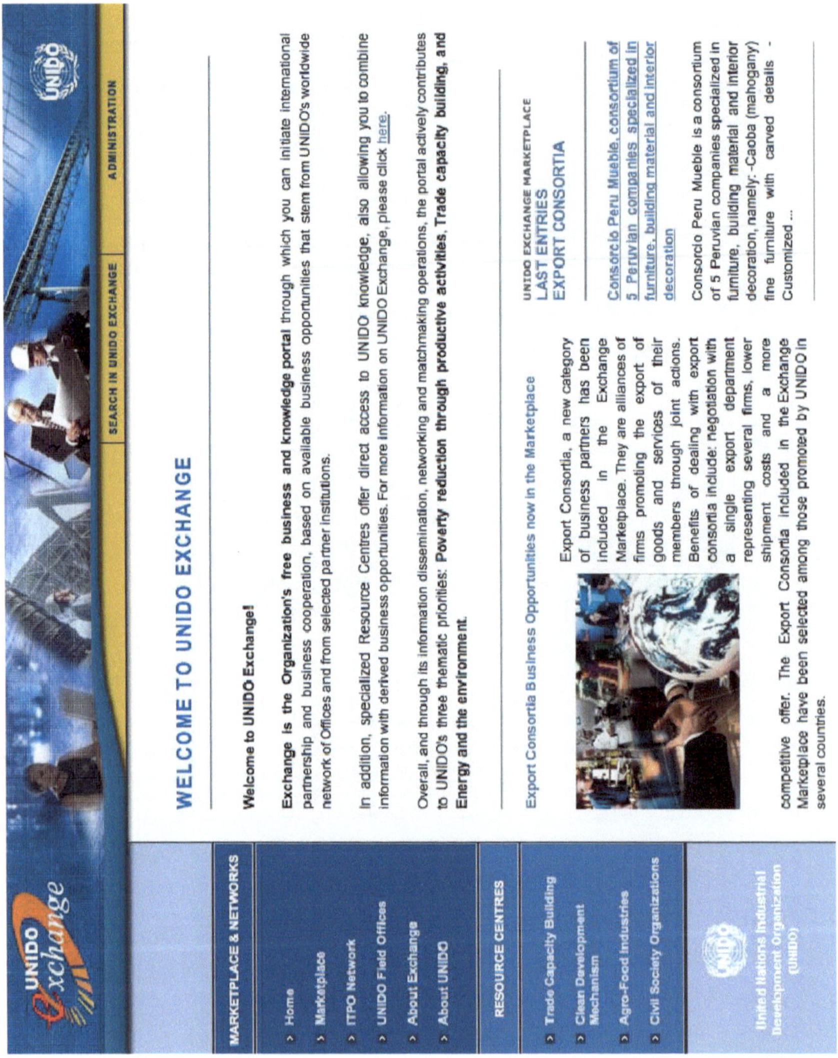

Figure 2.14: UNIDO exchange welcome page

Search Page

UNIDO Exchange

ADMINISTRATION

SEARCH IN UNIDO EXCHANGE

MARKETPLACE & NETWORKS

> Home
> Marketplace
> ITPO Network
> UNIDO Field Offices
> About Exchange
> About UNIDO

RESOURCE CENTRES

> Research and Statistics
> Trade Capacity Building
> Clean Development Mechanism
> Agro-Food Industries
> Civil Society Organizations

Search in Marketplace databases

Search for marketplace items containing: [   ] GO

Search the following databases:

· Investment and Cooperation Opportunities
· Technology Opportunities
· Product Offers and Requests

Search complete UNIDO Exchange portal

Search for pages containing: [   ] GO

Search the entire portal, including following Resource Centres and Sub-Sites:

· Agro-Food Industries
· Civil Society and Non-Governmental Organizations
· Strategy and Research
· Trade Capacity Building Initiative
· Mediterranean Exchange
· UNIDO Investment Promotion Unit Jordan

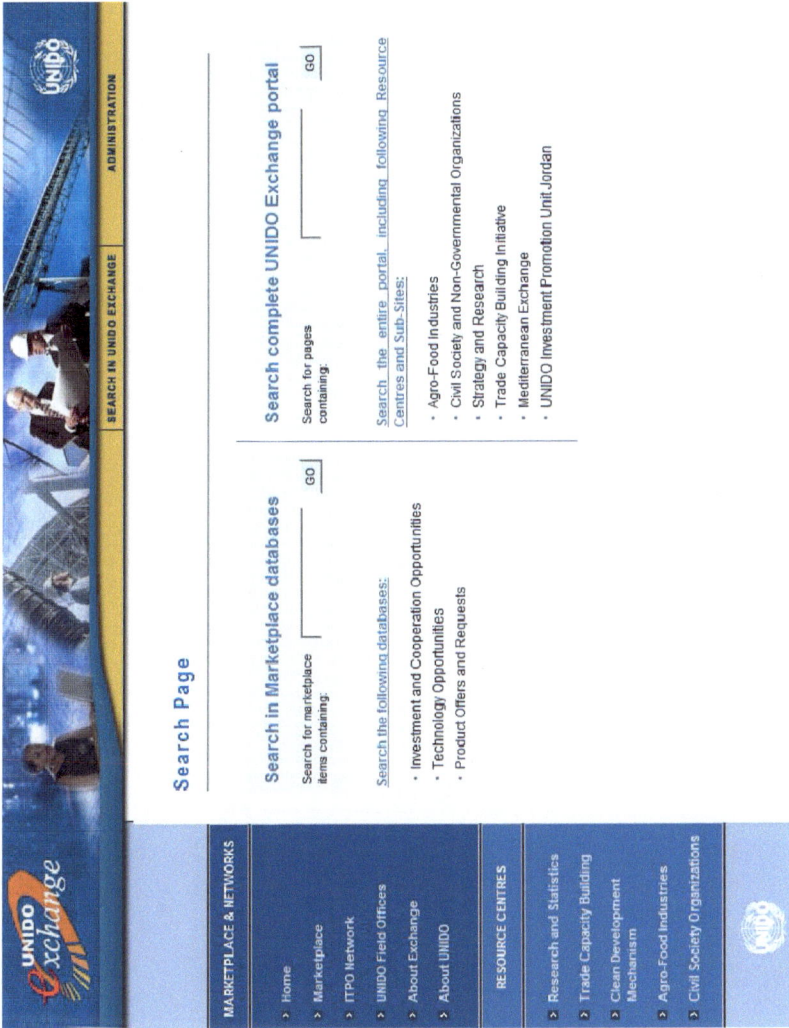

Figure 2.15: UNIDO Exchange portal search page

Figure 2.16: UNIDO Exchange portal

The social capital of the organization was enhanced by the refinement of the thematic priorities of the organization. These priorities included, (1) trade capacity-building, (2) poverty reduction through productive activities in non-farm sectors and, (3) energy and environment, mapped directly to the MDG [45, 88] and the UNIDO integrated program portfolio [116]. It also created the opportunity for the organization to collaborate with other funds and programs within the UN system to meet the MDG. UNIDO signed a number of co-operative agreements with other organizations, including UNCTAD, UNDP, UNFIP, and UNEP in order to avoid duplication, pooling resources for improved collaboration in capacity-building projects.

2.7 UNODC STORYLINE

During the Cold War, the greatest concern of the United Nations was the international war. Today, the international community is more preoccupied with intra-state or religious conflicts, terrorism, domestic and trans-national crime [117]. The work of the UNODC has expanded to meet some of these issues. The UNODC provides leadership in the fight against illicit drugs and international crime by assisting member countries in the ratification and implementation of international treaties and in the development of domestic legislation on drugs, crime and terrorism. It also conducts research and technical cooperation activities to enhance the capacity of member countries to counteract illicit drugs, crime and terrorism.

As a substantive department of the United Nations, a part of the United Nations office in Vienna, the UNODC has grown significantly since its creation in 1957. It now operates in nearly 70 countries and has 35 field offices. As a result of this organic growth, the organization faced challenges in managing its resources effectively. For example, in the 1990s it could not adequately account for the number of international staff on its payroll. There was also very little disclosure of progress of projects, budgets and expenditure. Internally, the need for effective resource management drove change towards the use of IT for automating many of its processes. Externally, due to a lack of transparency in its budgets, expenditure and projects, the organization was finding it more difficult to attract funds from member countries for its programs.

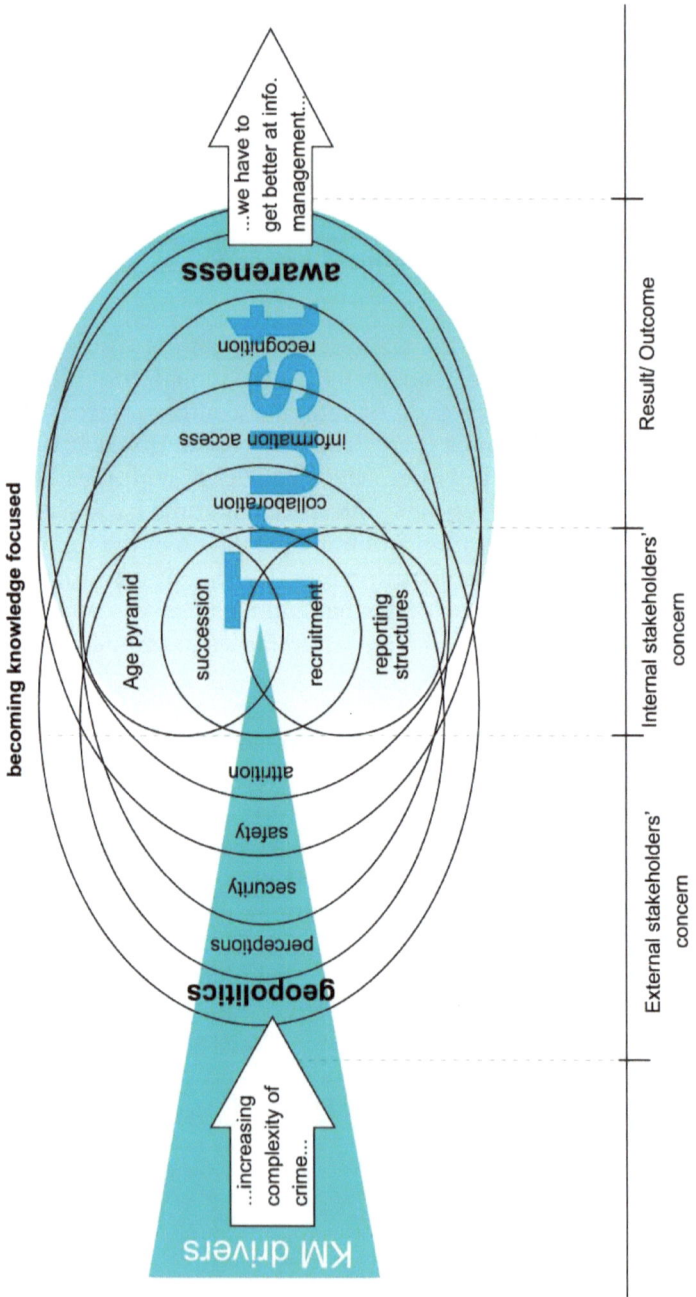

Figure 2.17: Relationship of categories and core category for UNODC

EXTERNAL KM CHALLENGES

In UNODC, the external context revolved around the increasing complexity of international organized crime, including drug trafficking, trafficking in human beings, trafficking in firearms, smuggling of migrants, money laundering, and the need to raise awareness among governments and citizens "…traditional hierarchical forms of organized crime groups have diminished; replaced with loose networks who work together in order to exploit weaknesses in national and international law enforcement frameworks…" Requests for assistance in the implementation of international treaties and in the development of domestic legislation, particularly by developing countries, have meant that the organization has had to expand its normative and operational functions to nearly 70 countries, opening offices in 35 countries.

INTERNAL KM CHALLENGES

The challenges faced by the UNODC were firstly to consolidate the disparate systems and databases and to replace them with distributed replicated architectures. Secondly, it had to change the organizational culture from papyrocentric to enabling people to use computerized systems. Although there were filing systems for hard copies, they proved inadequate to cope with growing numbers of activities of the organization.

KM INTERVENTIONS

The UNODC started to focus on its knowledge assets by implementing a number of computerized systems, used by a wide variety of clients. These software systems included Enterprise Resource Planning (ERP), known as the Programme and Financial Information Management System (ProFi) (cf. Figure 2.18), providing financial (pledges, collections, budgets, expenditures) and substantive (project ideas, documents, progress reports, evaluations) information and services for drugs and crime projects executed by UNODC [118]. Governments, financial and crimes bodies around the world now interface with the UNODC systems from the headquarters or any of its 35 field offices.

Internally, the shift from a papyrocentric to more computerized systems was led by the IT unit and was also endorsed by the UNODC management. The IT unit upgraded its infrastructure, consolidating databases into a common repository in Lotus Notes© and developed a distributed architecture to serve its field offices. In this case, the distributed architecture was designed to be fully redundant-- in other words, local offices work within their local area network (LAN) and data is synchronized at set intervals, behind the scenes with the headquarters systems. This ensured that everyone worked with high speed access in their context.

Figure 2.18: UNODC Programme and Financial Information system (ProFi)

Lotus Notes© was used as the main interface and transport layer for replicating and distributing data stored in the PROFI system. Training and support was given to staff and it was mandated that all processes of the organization were to start in the new computerized portal system. Storing of records on network and personal drives, as well as sending hard copies or email attachments, was discouraged as part of the management policy. Form driven workflow systems were used to start processes and exchange information with the organization. Classification and archiving of information was automated with little or no human intervention once a document was uploaded with associated metadata. The strategy was to "ensure that all data and processes were stored in the same place—in the line of process".

In order to help build capacity in member countries, enabling them to implement international treaties, the technical cooperation programs collaborated with the IT unit to write software programs that can be used to monitor and report on criminal activities, such as applications for monitoring money laundering and so on.

2.8 EU STORYLINE

The EU storyline is focused on 2006, and particularly during the second Austrian Presidency—January to June 2006. The EU presidency rotates among the EU Member states, following a predetermined order. Austria held the presidency once before in 1998 and is scheduled to hold it again in 2019. The key strategic issues for the Austrian Presidency were set out in the EU council's 2004-2006 multi annual strategic programme [119]. Austria and Finland, which held the presidency in 2006, used this plan as a basis for establishing their detailed operational and normative activities in 2006.

In becoming knowledge focused in the EU, progression was from an initial critical phase, described by chief coordinators of the Austrian EU presidency as "growing euroscepticism". This growing sentiment was exacerbated by the rejection of the EU constitutional treaty in France and the Netherlands. Therefore, a major objective of the Austrian EU presidency was to try to win back trust and confidence in the EU.

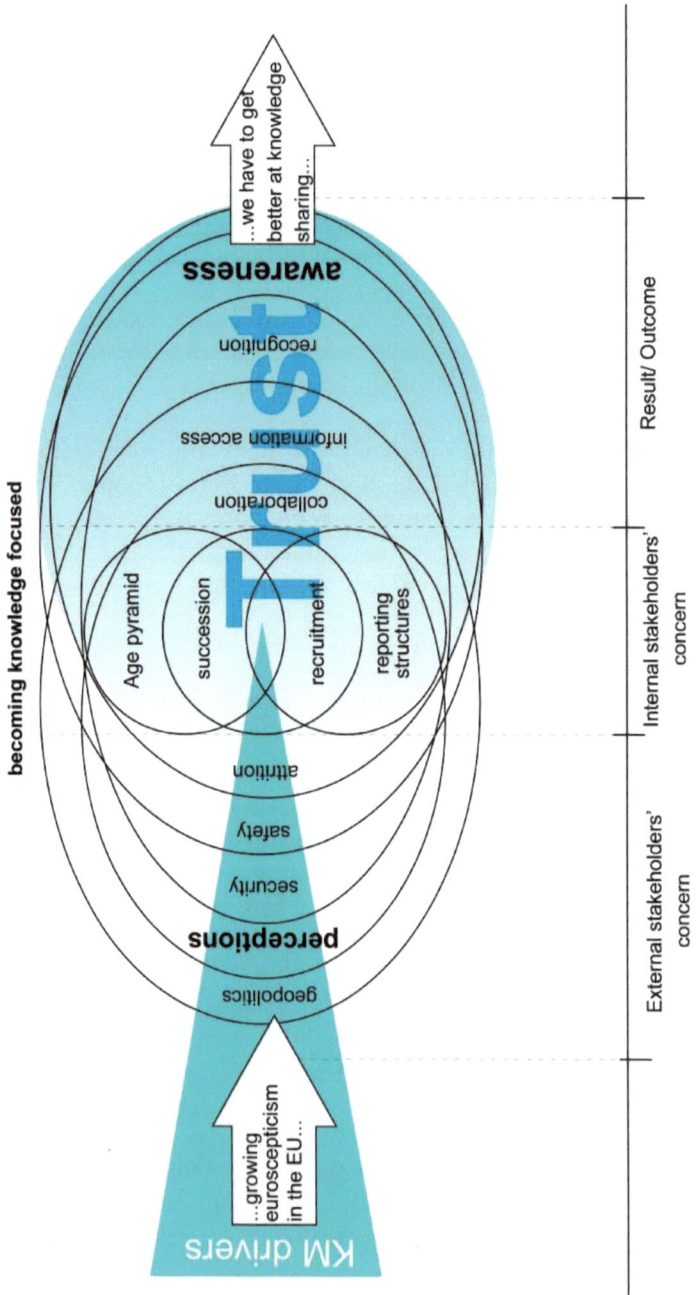

Figure 2.19: Relationship of categories and core category for the EU

EXTERNAL KNOWLEDGE MANAGEMENT CHALLENGES

In the EU, the external context revolved around public perception among Europeans that the EU was incapable of delivering concrete results that could positively affect their daily lives. These external perceptions were exacerbated by a broad range of geopolitical concerns that had succeeded past EU leaderships, ranging from, (a) the low productivity and stagnation of economic growth among much of Europe, (b) rejection of the EU constitutional treaty by the Dutch and French, (c) enlargement of the EU to the Balkans, (d) lack of consensus over the EU budget to, (e) consensus over Iran's nuclear ambitions and, (f) the growing threat of bird flu.

INTERNAL KNOWLEDGE MANAGEMENT CHALLENGES

The internal context of the EU presidency revolved around a three-year strategic program containing the following objectives (2004 to 2006)[119]:

- Create jobs and growth in Europe
- Secure and develop specifically a European social model
- Rebuild confidence in the European project among EU citizens
- Further establish Europe as a strong and reliable partner

These objectives were developed in consideration of the views of all member countries and served as a starting point for establishing the detailed operational programme of the Austrian presidency.

Given the political climate of Euro-scepticism, the Austrian presidency faced the challenge of communicating these objectives to European citizens in an attractive manner. Thus the personal goals of the presidency was (1) how to build trust by establishing a debate with citizens on the vague concept of the European identity and (2) how to strengthen cross border collaboration, particularly in the areas of research.

KNOWLEDGE MANAGEMENT INTERVENTIONS

At the macro level, the Austrian presidency tackled the issues of research by focusing on enhancing the intellectual capital of Europe by revitalizing the Lisbon treaty [120]—the vision to create a competitive knowledge based economy in Europe.

...to become the most competitive and dynamic knowledge-based economy in the world capable of sustainable economic growth with more and better jobs and greater social cohesion...

The Lisbon strategy [120] is an action plan set out by the European Council in Lisbon on March 2000. The three pillars of the strategy advice member countries to focus on, (1) boosting research to enable a more completive, dynamic knowledge based economy, (2) investing in education and training and to conduct an active policy for employment, making it easier to move towards a knowledge economy and, (3) decoupling of economic growth from the use of natural resources [121].

In order to meet the objectives of the Lisbon strategy, the EU council approved the 53 billion Euro Research Framework Program (FP7) and budget at the end of 2006 [122], representing a 63% increase from the earlier research framework programme FP6 budget (cf. Figure 2.20).

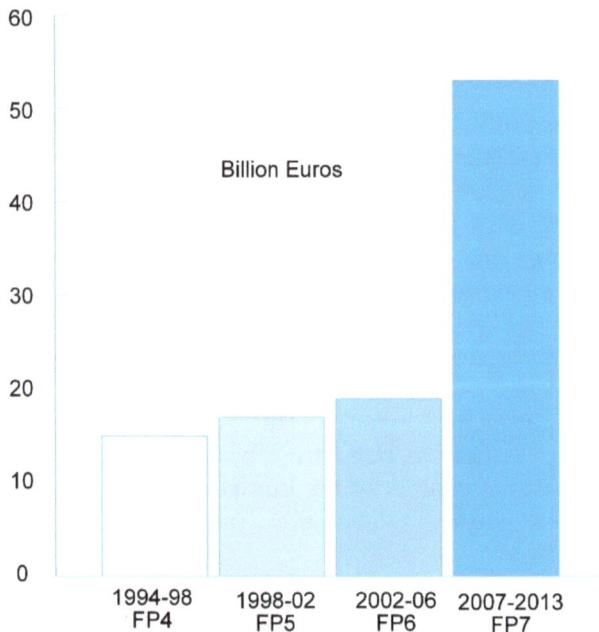

Figure 2.20: Evolution of EU Research Framework Programme Budgets

The FP7 priorities included the creation of communities of researchers across Europe (cooperation programme) around key research themes, as well as support for cutting edge research (ideas programme) outside the thematic areas. These thematic areas included health; food, agriculture and fisheries, and biotechnology; information and communications technologies; nano-sciences, nanotechnologies, materials and new production technologies; energy; environment (including climate change); transport (including aeronautics); socio-economic sciences and the humanities; space and security. The ideas program was the first time that the EU framework research program (FP) included pure investigative research at the frontiers of science and technology, independently of the thematic areas.

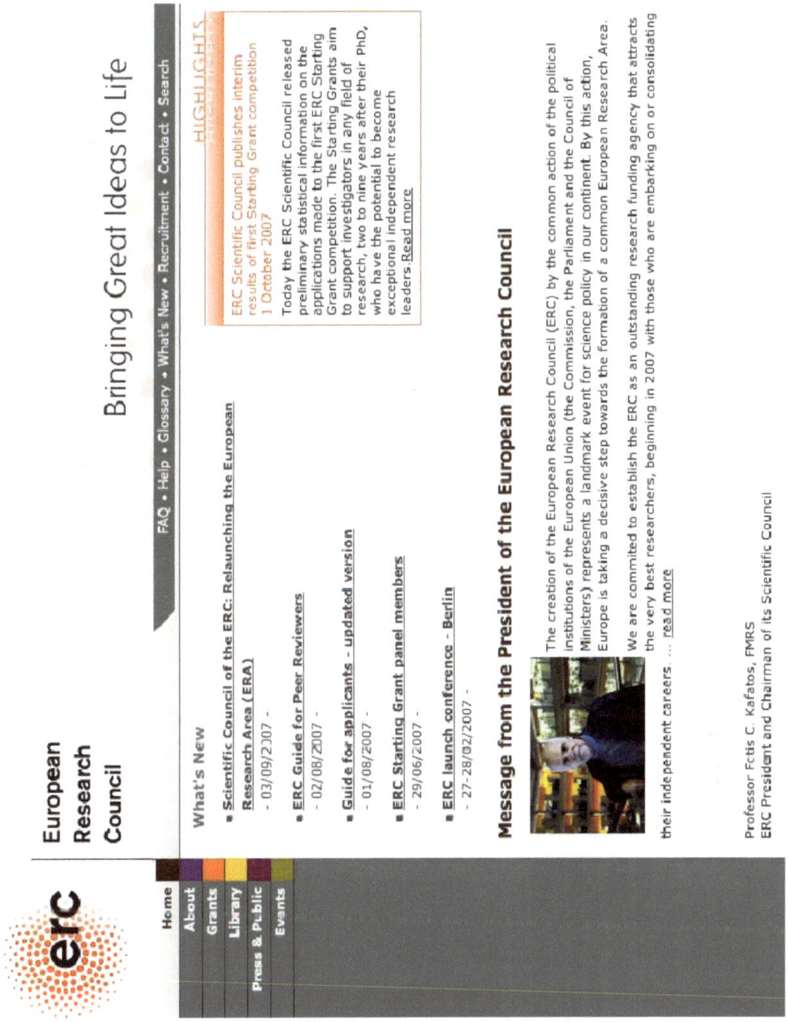

Figure 2.21: European research council website

Figure 2.22 Community Research & Development Information Service (CORDIS)

In order to improve trust and confidence in the European project, several forums for debate were created by the Austrian presidency. Programs such as "Europe listens", "Sound of Europe" (a debate on European identity), and "Café d' Europe" (cf. Figure 2.23), were set up, some forums had websites, live streaming, and email and hotlines services, used to reach out to citizens.

Stories of Europe | Initiative for Europe Day 2006 | www.cafeeurope.at

institut der **regionen europas**

EU | AT

Home | Imprint

The Stories of Europe | The Europe Journal | Sweet Europe | Press Contact | Downloads | Initiators | Sponsors

Café d'Europe
09 | 05 | 2006

"The café is a place for meetings and conspiracies, for intellectual debates and talks. If one were to draw a map of the coffeehouses, one would have the general outline of the European idea...." - George Steiner, Cicero

For Europe Day 2006, on 9 May, the Institute of the Regions of Europe (IRE) launched a cultural project across Europe backed by the Austrian Presidency of the Council of the EU – the Café d'Europe.

Café d'Europe.

Cafés, perhaps more than any other institution, stand for communication and local culture. They are a symbol of our common European heritage.

Café d'Europe

Europe is listening.

In 27 Cafés d'Europe, in 27 European capitals, coffeehouse discussions took place on Europe Day with the public and young people from all over Europe. Questions were asked, ideas aired, creative and visionary approaches proposed. The core issue of this discussion was – and still is – the diversity and colourful nature of the European Union.

In the Cafés d'Europe people – writers and members of the public – had the chance to write their "Story of Europe". Everyone is still welcome to hand in his or her story via this website.

Europe. Be inspired.

Participating Cafès

Click the info button 🛈 for event details.

Austria Vienna	**Café Central** Herrengasse 14	1010 Wien Austria	🛈
Belgium Brussels	**Café Falstaff** 17-21 rue Henri Mausstraat	Brussels Belgium	🛈
Bulgaria Sofia	**Café Bulgaria, Grand Hotel Bulgaria** 4 Tzar Osvoboditel Blvd.	Sofia 1000 Bulgaria	🛈
Cyprus Nikosia	**Flo Café** 132 - 134 Ledras street	Nikosia Cyprus	🛈
Czech Republic Prague	**Café Slavia** Narodni trida Nr. 1/1012	Praha 1, 11 000 Czech Republic	🛈
Denmark Copenhagen	**Café Sommersko** Kronprinsensgade 6	1114 København K Denmark	🛈
Estonia Tallinn	**Kohvik Bestseller** Viru Väljak 4/6, Viru Keskuse 3.korus	10123 Tallinn Estonia	🛈
Finland Helsinki	**Kappeli** Eteläesplanadi 1	00130 Helsinki Finland	🛈
France Paris	**Café Les Duex Magots** 6 place Saint Germain des Prés	75006 Paris France	🛈
Germany Berlin	**Café Einstein** Kurfürstenstraße 58	10785 Berlin Germany	🛈
Greece Athens	**Café Ianos** Stadiou 24	Athens, 105 64 Greece	🛈
Hungary Budapest	**Centrál Kávéház** Károlyi Mihály u. 9.	1053 Budapest Hungary	🛈

Sweet Europe

Europe. Be seduced.

Downloads

Participating cafés (PDF 130KB)

Figure 2.23: Café d' Europe websites

2.9 CONCLUSION

All international organizations are expected to serve as a repository of technical expertise for its member countries, serving its member countries and regional commissions, as well as other international organizations and in this capacity advise them on various questions of international and national significance. Conceptually, issues faced by international organizations were similar, based on their functions.

Mandate overlap was recognized as part of the drivers for becoming knowledge-focused in operationally oriented organizations (cf. Figure 2.25) but not a driver in normative oriented organizations (cf. Figure 2.24). Whereas normative oriented organizations focus on other matters that drive KM efforts, related to global security, safety, and so on (cf. Figure 2.24), the internal drivers and outcomes reported were similar in international organizations with a normative and operational orientation.

International organizations are non-profit oriented and by nature have a significant purpose of trust, made explicit in their respective mandates. Trust is vital for knowledge management [70] and is needed for influencing multilateral actors in international organizations. Thus, trust was seen as the enabling condition for the organizations to manage knowledge, both internally and externally (cf. Figure 2.25 and Figure 2.24).

Factors which affected the progression were the mediating factors, or intervening conditions, identified in the axial coding (cf. Appendix B) — that is, KM depended on political will and trust at the micro and macro levels, as well as the organizations' ability to influence stakeholder behaviour, encourage collaboration and build capacity. These findings are discussed in greater detail in the following chapter— in relation to the idiosyncratic issues of KM in international organizations (cf. Section 1.6).

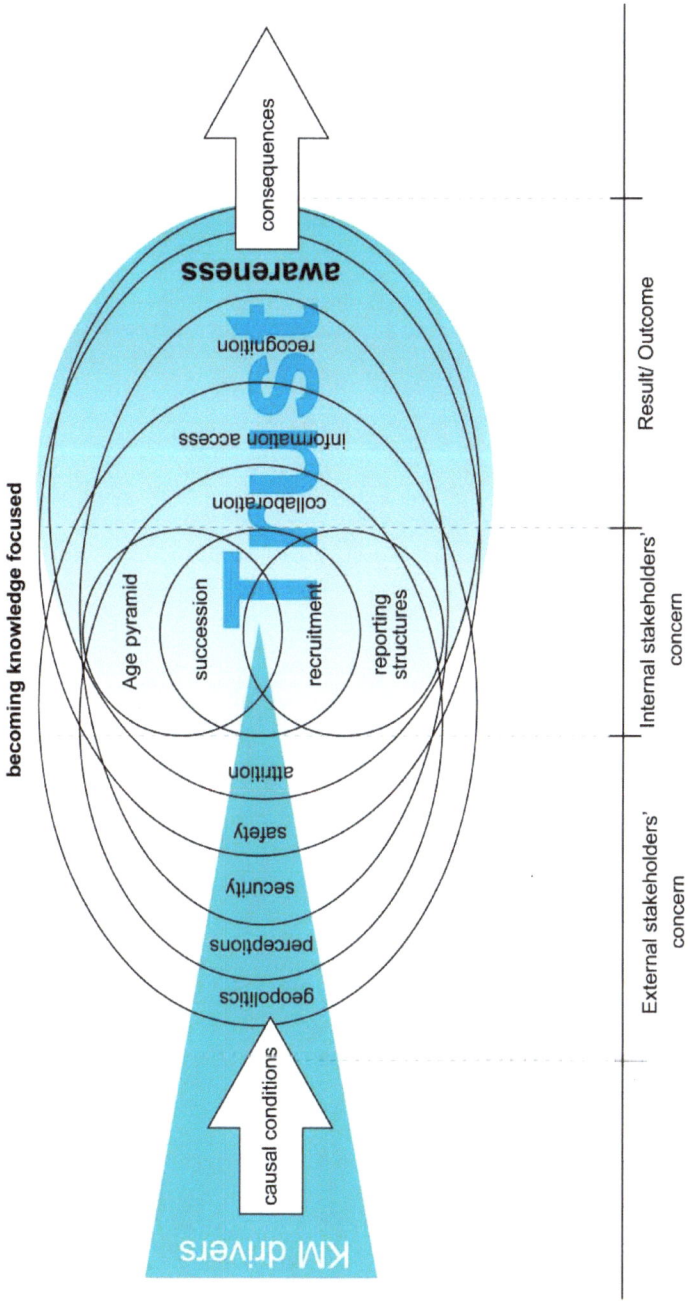

Figure 2.24: Relationship of categories for normative functions

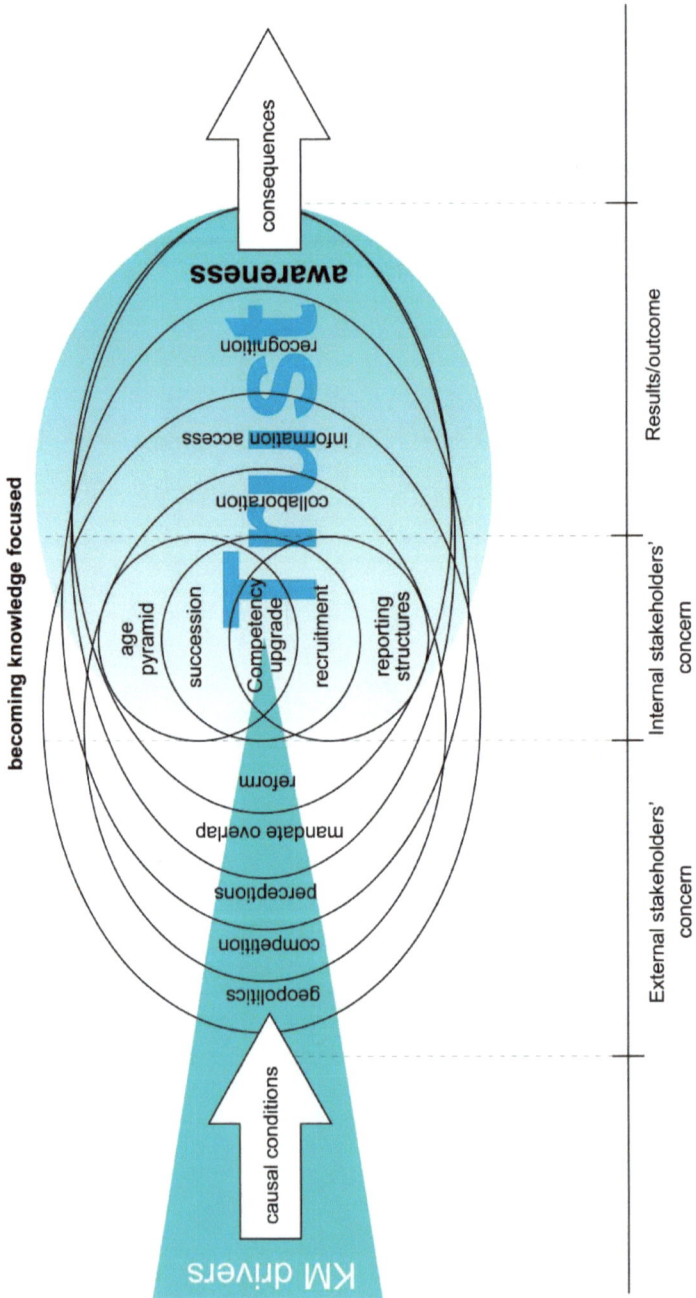

Figure 2.25: Relationship of categories for operational functions

CHAPTER 3
FACTORS INVOLVED IN
MANAGING KNOWLEDGE

Knowledge can be categorized at the basic level into explicit and tacit [71]. It is also the result of a human activity at the individual and group level [69]. However, in international organizations, knowledge management involves both interpersonal activities of professionals and impersonal activities of countries, made explicit by their representatives. Thus knowledge management in international organizations is characterized by explicit activities and implicit factors — activities that can be observed, as well as those factors that lie hidden behind the scenes.

Collaboration and capacity-building can be seen as dimensions of the organization's functions (normative and operational) (cf. Figure 3.1 and Appendix A for definitions of the concepts) and, therefore, can be described as the explicit factors. In practice, these observable factors place entirely different demands on the management and governing structure of the organization, depending on its functions. For example, the fulfilment of normative functions requires universal participation and formal equality among all participants. Inherent in norm setting is the need to reach out and increase the number and diversity of the actors, in order to ensure international support for new normative functions. For example, following the rejection of the EU constitution in France and the Netherlands, the Austrian presidency utilized several outreach programmes to share knowledge with the citizens of Europe in an attempt to win back confidence in the European project (cf. Section 2.8).

Operational function requires a structure and management culture that promotes decision-making capabilities, as the organization shares the problem of implementing policy decisions. Moreover, the operational functions are judged on their effectiveness in achieving capacity building objectives with the resources at their disposal. UNIDO was forced to downsize its operations and budget in part because of perceptions of inefficacy, particularly among donor countries (cf. Section 2.6).

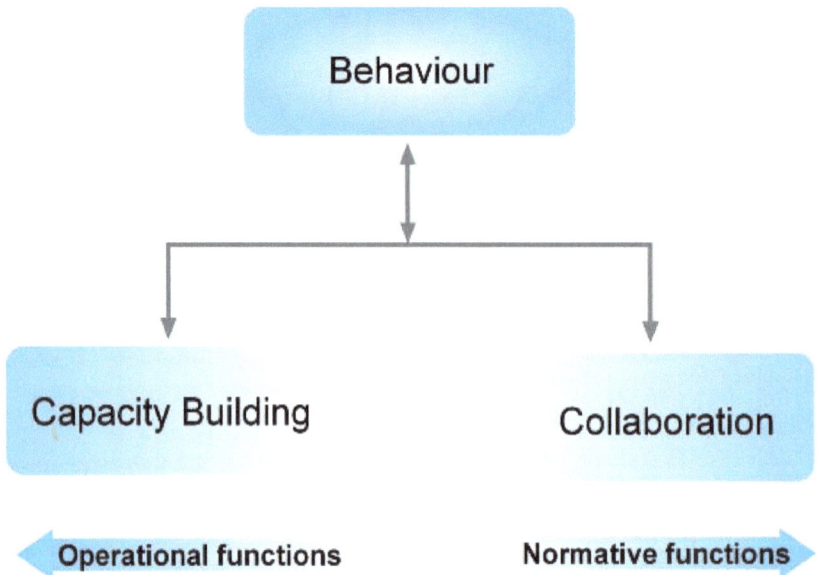

Figure 3.1: Factors involved in KM in international organizations

Stakeholder behaviour, the observable actions of stakeholders, can be better understood from the perspective of the implicit factors, such as trust, politics, stakeholder interaction and leadership. These implicit factors are described in the following sections.

3.1 TRUST

The probability that a stakeholder will share knowledge with other stakeholders—collaborating or building capacity (Figure 3.1)—is dependent on politics and the levels of trust in the structure of relations between stakeholders and the organization, including at least calculative trust [123], which the stakeholder perceives in such an interaction (cf. Equation 5.1).

$$v_b = v_{b-1} + \varepsilon_b$$

Equation 3.1: Stakeholder calculative trust equation

Equation 3.1 illustrates that the value of a new knowledge-sharing behaviour (v_b) is equal to the value of the previous behaviour (v_{b-1}), plus or minus motivation (ε_b), a variable representing the self-interest of the stakeholder. The assumption is that if every stakeholder acted *"rationally"* in the absence of an appreciation of at least calculative trust (cf. Table 3.1), no stakeholder would cooperate, resulting in collective suboptimal or Paraeto-inefficient outcomes[2] (cf. Figure 3.2: quadrant B and D). Figure 3.2 below characterizes the different outcomes of stakeholder (member country) relations with an international organization.

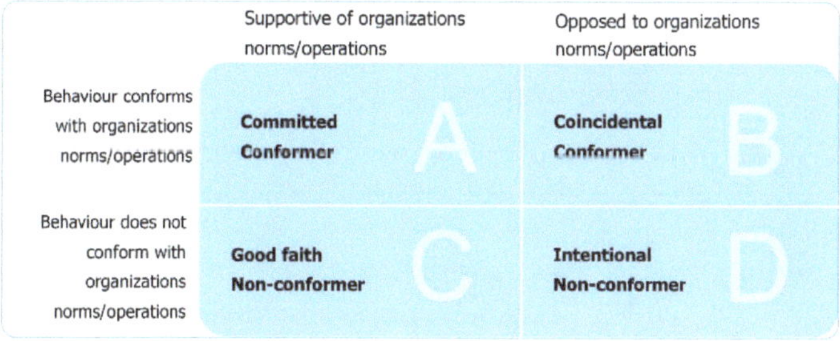

Figure 3.2: Trust relations in international organizations (Adapted from: [124])

[2] An outcome is Pareto-efficient if and only if there exists no other outcome that (1) leaves any actor better off and (2) leaves no actor worse

The **committed conformer (quadrant A)** represents those stakeholders (member countries) that facilitate the organizations normative and operational functions. For example, although all countries support the UN Millennium Development Goals (MDG) [88], fewer countries, excluding the Canada, USA and Australia, are committed to supporting international interventions through UNIDO, due to individual country interests [13].

The **intentional non conformer (quadrant D)** represents those stakeholders (member countries), that intentionally do not support the organizations goals [124]. For example, the effectiveness of the IAEA's KM processes in the area of nuclear safeguards and inspections in Iraq was intentionally undermined by the lack of cooperation and trust among actors, leading to war.

The **good faith non conformer (quadrant C)** represents those stakeholders that support the organization, but fall short of its norms and standards because of incapacity or inadvertence. IMO's technical cooperation programme [125] helps developing countries in the IMO build capacity to comply with international norms and standards relating to maritime safety, and the prevention and control of maritime pollution.

Coincidental Conformer (quadrant B) includes stakeholders that are either indifferent or opposed to the organizations goals, but whose behaviour conforms for reasons other than commitment [124]. Although opposed to international organizations functions, they selectively conform to particular functions if the organization offers instrumental benefits. The rise of neoconservative movement in US politics and, in particular, the concepts of "preventive/pre-emptive war"[126], threatens the relevancy of international organizations functions in achieving world peace, security and development.

Understanding motivational factors therefore, is vital for managing knowledge in international organizations—even though the organization may not be sufficiently empowered (cf. Section 4.2) to transform its stakeholders into committed conformers (cf. Figure 3.2).

For all stakeholders, the calculative trust forms the basis of relations and the basic means of soliciting intelligent cooperation. However, cognitive trust [123] is less dependent on a calculation as depicted in calculative trust (cf. Table 3.1), and, therefore, can only be developed through sharing common cognitions between the parties concerned [123]. This sharing of cognitions can provide a basis for understanding (and possibly predicting) the actions of stakeholders, based on shared expectations. Member countries of OPEC benefit from unifying their petroleum policies, in spite of challenges facing individual countries.

The main motivating factors that can influence outcomes, shown in Figure 3.2, is different for normative and operational functions, as depicted in Table 3.1.

Table 3.1: Trust relations in international organizations

	Knowledge workers	Operational functions	Normative functions
Calculative trust (ε_b)	• Benefits compensation • Career path • Job security • Staff rules • Payoffs for contributing • Efficacy perceptions	• Balance of power • Political agendas of stakeholders • Benefits from brokered international intervention in recipient countries • Benefits from continued international cooperation • A sense of status	• Balance of power • Political agendas of stakeholders Avoidance of internationally • imposed penalties for non-compliance • Benefits from continued international cooperation A sense of status
Cognitive trust	• Trust in the mandate of the organization • Trust in the expertise of individuals in the organization • Personal responsibility	• Trust relations between the member countries and the organization to understand the needs, interests and priorities in technical cooperation projects	• Principle of equality among member countries • Trust in the normative rules decided upon collectively by member countries
Trust building interactions with the organization	• Expertise recognition • Community of practice • Mentorship • Exit interviewing • Encouraging socialization • Maintaining a quota of culturally diverse experts from member countries • Knowledge audits, and IC reporting	• Deployment of authoritative expertise • Quality of project proposal • Sustainable projects as a result of knowledge transfer from organization to country • Positive outcome of projects implemented (results based management)	• Providing unbiased information, based on research • Providing a platform for dialogue and networking • Strategically increasing diversity of actors, in order to ensure support for new normative functions

← **interpersonal relations**   **Impersonal relations** →

A third view of trust is identification-based [127], involving culture and associated language and political idiosyncrasies that can impede communication. For example, not all IAEA nuclear inspectors are accredited to all countries, and sometimes collaboration between experts and stakeholders in a country requires the aid of translators—

who are not subject matter experts themselves. This multilingual context of operations is exacerbated by the number of official working languages managed by international organizations—the EU maintains over 23 official languages. Maintaining a culturally diverse pool of specialists from different regions of the world is important for operational and normative functions, in order to build identification-based trust.

3.1.1   ORGANIZATIONAL LEADERSHIP

At the organizational level, the difference between normative and operational power (cf. Section 4.2) can be viewed in terms of leadership versus management responsibility. In the light of the volatile and high profile working conditions in international organizations, it is important to distinguish the role of leaders, (for example, the Secretary or Director General (or equivalent high-level post). The leader's role is to continue to motivate and inspire the organization's staff [128]. By inspiring and motivating staff members, the leader keeps employees working in the right direction. Management, on the other hand, has greater responsibility for carrying out the vision of the leader. The "one house" concept, a shared value [129], preached by the IAEA Director General, was used as a tool to try to shape the corporate culture at the Agency by influencing his management team "to embrace cross-cutting programs and projects". In UNIDO, the Director General has also been instrumental in influencing the behaviour of stakeholders. For example, in a memo dated 18th October, 2006, entitled "communication and information-sharing between staff", he encouraged staff to be more open—"to show signs of knowledge sharing". The Director General effectively lead managers in UNIDO to create an international mobility policy, encouraging staff to rotate between field offices, as one form of career advancement. Thematic groups across the organization, like the value chain analysis group, and the energy efficiency group, were identified and formalized into the organizations structure in 2006.

Externally, the DG is in a far more complex web of interaction with influential others (cf. Figure 1.1) than any organization chart can suggest. The DG seeks to unite member countries, consulting informally with key officials and key delegations when making recommendations on important knowledge-management issues, just as member countries seek to resolve their differences in reaching a consensus. For example, at the governmental level, the cutbacks in government spending (stakeholder behaviour) in the nuclear industry, following the deregulation of energy markets in the 1990s, exacerbated the attrition rate of technical competence in the nuclear industry, including at the Agency, more than any other factor. Thus, influencing the behaviour of governments to reverse this trend is made possible by reporting the issues to the member countries (cf. see Dr. Mohamed Elbaradei's statement on page 26) and organizing international conferences on nuclear KM, where communities of interest to the organization, such as academia, related industry specialists and government officials can participate and share best practices. The Director General's leadership in issues areas is thus a *sine qua non* for effective KM [130-132].

3.1.2 POLITICS

All international organizations studied had political inefficiencies built into the system of governance and management that limited knowledge sharing potential in different ways. For example, in operationally-oriented organizations, policies simultaneously required the organization and individuals within the organization to compete and, at the same time, collaborate with others for resources. At the macro level, co-determinant politics encourage collaboration where there is potential for mandate overlap. Organizations like UNIDO, OSCE and OFID depend on idiosyncratic expert knowledge (cf. Section 1.2.3), as well as a coalition of other operationally oriented organizations in order to effectively deliver benefits that can effect change in recipient countries. The Global Environmental Facility (GEF) [133], a financial institution, includes many operational-oriented organizations as implementing[133] and executing agencies [134], such as UNDP, UNEP, World Bank, AFDB, ADB, EBRD, IDB, IFAD, FAO and UNIDO. Co-determinacy creates a climate for potential mandate overlap in operational activities, as well as the resulting competition for limited resources.

Normative functions rely on bureaucracy; in the sense that the use of the written word provides for a rational type of authority [135]. At the macro level, ratification "on paper" of international agreements by countries provides for normative influence on individual governments--whereas implementation of the agreements is left to the sovereign countries.

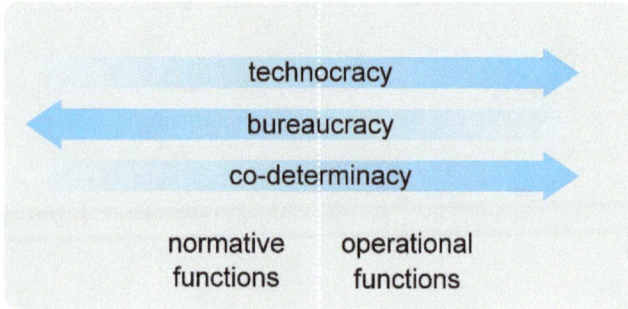

Figure 3.3: Modes of politics

At the organizational level, information and knowledge dissemination is influenced by external politics. For example, electronic records management systems (ERM) in the IAEA ensure that security policies are strictly adhered to. Information is controlled in such a way that security classifications and personnel clearances are complicated by an additional requirement described as "the need to know". This requirement involves the implementation of special classes that define small categories of personnel who are able to view specific records according to their role within the organization and their relationship to a specific project and even nationality. Nuclear inspectors in the IAEA have access only to records and projects, based on their accreditation to a particular country, their nationality and their direct involvement in a particular project.

Information security is not new [136-138], but what is new is the way in which it is implemented in the context of international organizations. Organizations like the IAEA, UNODC, OPEC and IMO have had to customize off-the-shelf ERM and document management packages, or develop entirely new systems to handle the complex relational requirements of their records and information management.

A knowledge manager in an international organization needs to be aware of how these political factors impact knowledge management initiatives, with a view to taking informed decisions.

3.2 KNOWLEDGE PRODUCTS AND SERVICES

The knowledge flows between stakeholders and international organizations can be categorized into three interrelated products and services: project management, expertise, and advice. A hierarchical depiction of the knowledge products and services, the results of knowledge flows, are shown below (Figure 3.4), juxtaposed against KM strategy [5], and organizational functions.

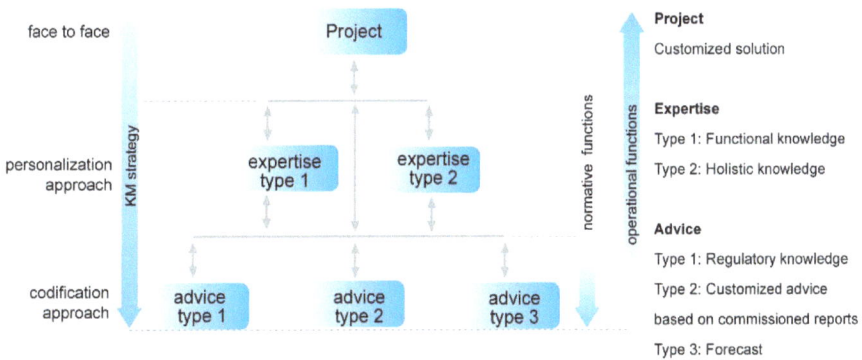

Figure 3.4: Knowledge products and service request hierarchy

Project requests, at the top of the hierarchy in Figure 3.4, imply strategy formulation: assessing a country's strengths, weaknesses and opportunities and threats related to the request. The Master Plan for the development of the Ethiopian leather and leather products industry, produced jointly by UNIDO and the Government of Ethiopia, were adopted as a key part of Ethiopian strategic framework for industrial development in 2005 [139]. The emphasis of the Master Plan included the ability to access regional and global markets; potential for value addition; job creation and income generation; and the potential to attract domestic and foreign investment.

Requests for expertise (cf. type 1 or 2) require transferring specialists across national boundaries. For example, specialists (and funds) from Italy provided technical assistance through UNIDO to help build the managerial and operational capacity of stakeholders in the Leather industry in Ethiopia—mainly through training and technology transfer programmes. The competencies of these specialists (cf. expertise type 1 or 2) are managed by the organization in a database.

A request for advice (cf. type 2) can be the result of a commissioned project request, where as an outcome of feasibility studies, other related issues/sectors are identified. In OPEC's Long Term Strategy [32], a scenario-approach for the energy scene is outlined, named respectively as: Dynamics-as Usual (DAU), Protracted Market Tightness (PMT), and Prolonged Soft Market (PSM). Each scenario envisages different possible futures where drivers of change in energy demand/supply differ. Such advice (cf. type 1 and 3) can also be codified (although not always the case), in the sense that member countries officials have access to international organizations' websites, intranets and knowledge portals, where they can search for needed information.

Stakeholder requests (cf. advice type 1, 2 and 3) of a normative oriented organization are a result of geopolitical concerns related to the organization's mandate. These can be categorized into general public concerns (media, academics, industry etc) and member country concerns. To address such concerns, the use of explicit knowledge (cf. advice type 1, 2 and 3) (treaties, research, commissioned reports, agreements, etc.), is needed to build consensus, influencing stakeholder behaviour and reaching new agreements, taking into consideration implicit factors such as calculative trust, as explained in Section 3.1.

3.3 TECHNOLOGY AND KNOWLEDGE MANAGEMENT

One of the ways international organizations answer the question of knowing what the organization knows (cf. Figure 4.2) is by using technology to represent knowledge, including who knows what. For operational functions like technical cooperation activities carried out in UNIDO, OSCE and OFID, a larger part of their substantive work is done in the field, including consultancy, project management and implementation support, requiring a greater degree of embodied, encultured and embrained knowledge [36] (cf. Section 1.2), and thus there is a greater need to use technology to connect people (cf. Figure 3.6, quadrants A, B and D) and thematic groups [140, 141]. UNIDO's knowledge portal, "The Exchange" (cf. Figure 2.15 and Figure 2.16) allows registered users to browse, search and find references to experts (people) within UNIDO's worldwide network of offices, and from selected partner institutions. Overall, the portal serves as a central point for information dissemination, networking and matchmaking operations. Efforts at codification of tacit knowledge in UNIDO are mainly for strategic planning and service improvement. The codification of knowledge is formally done by the Office for Strategy and Learning. Evaluators in the Office, interview project managers and related stakeholders in the field and attempt to derive lessons learned from projects at different stages of their life cycle. The information derived by the evaluators is actively disseminated throughout the organization via the presentations, the intranet, news letters, and on the website.

> *The rationale is that we should more rigorously do evaluations [of work carried out in the field]...to extract from them lessons learned and use those lessons learned to feed into our strategic planning...as a good feedback loop...*

In normative oriented international organizations like the IAEA, on the other hand, dealing mainly with embedded knowledge (cf. Section 2.1) — that is established nuclear scientific research, manuals and standards — there is a greater need to "preserve knowledge" (cf. see Dr. Mohamed Elbaradei's statement on page 26)—to house established scientific nuclear knowledge as it is for later generations. There is also pressure to try to standardize practices, particularly of experienced nuclear plant operators in the field in as much detail as possible. The IAEA also has a sophisticated records management system, based on the US Department of Defence standards for records keeping [142], with dedicated records management specialists, in addition to a document management system, used internally for working documents. The knowledge portal (INIS) houses a lot of content (cf. Figure 2.3) and focuses on helping researchers locate content, through complex searches (cf. Figure 2.2) and via the knowledge desk (cf. Figure 2.4). Therefore, relatively, there is a greater need for connecting people to documents for normative functions and a greater need for connecting people together for operational functions (cf. Figure 3.5, Figure 3.6)

On average, normative organizations in the sample had more demands on its information systems to help it manage explicit knowledge than operationally oriented organizations (cf. Figure 3.5). As discussed earlier (cf. Section 1.2), the types of knowledge used for normative and operational functions are different. Activities that are carried out to support normative functions are similar to secondary research (summarizing, collating and/or synthesis of existing information). Calculating the OPEC reference basket[3], involves an analysis of the following 12 crude oil prices from its member countries, including: Saharan Blend (Algeria), Girassol (Angola), Minas (Indonesia), Iran Heavy (Islamic Republic of Iran), Basra Light (Iraq), Kuwait Export (Kuwait), Es Sider (Libya), Bonny Light (Nigeria), Qatar Marine (Qatar), Arab Light (Saudi Arabia), Murban (UAE) and BCF 17 (Venezuela).

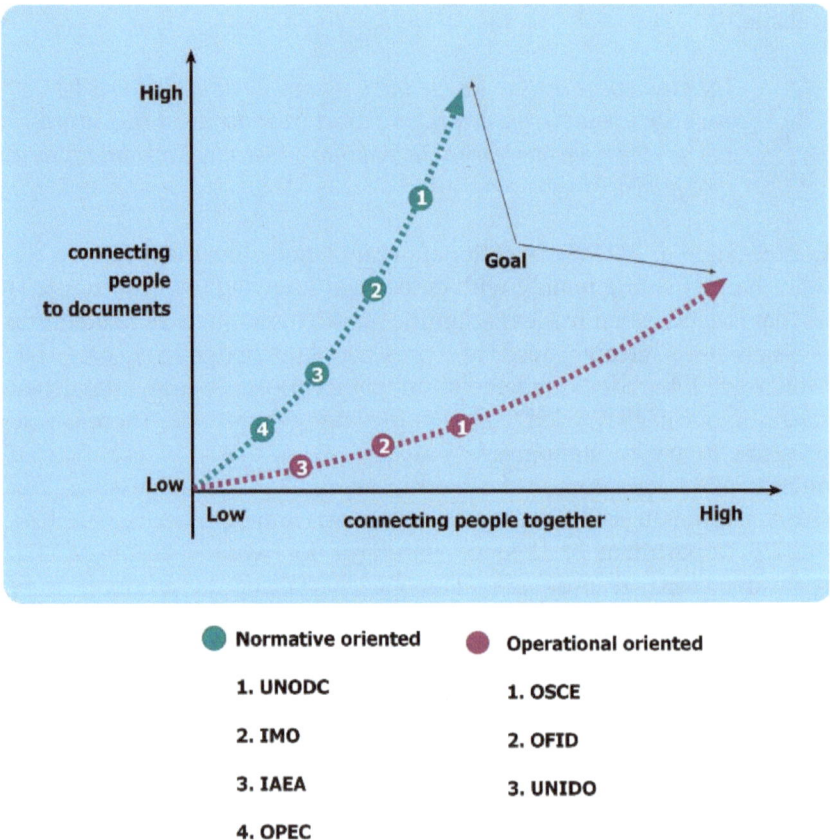

Normative oriented	Operational oriented
1. UNODC	1. OSCE
2. IMO	2. OFID
3. IAEA	3. UNIDO
4. OPEC	

Figure 3.5 Goal of technology strategy in normative and operational organizations

---

[3] Based on http://www.opec.org/home/basket.aspx

Activities that support operational functions are similar to primary research, (collecting and assessing data that does not already exist). Developing a Master Plan, as part of an operational function in UNIDO for industrial development of a particular country, involves face to face meetings, phone calls, video conferencing, and other technologies that can connect experts and stakeholders together.

For normative functions relying on secondary data, demands on technology include access to high quality databases, websites and the use of records management systems. In OPEC, data on world oil production and oil stock levels are a few of the kinds of data that researchers in OPEC require to do their work.

From the diagram in Figure 3.5, UNODC shows greatest demands on its Information Systems in both dimensions: to connect people together, as well as to connect people to documents. This can be explained by its diverse mix of functions—relative to the other organizations in the sample, the UNODC performs the most diverse mix of operational and normative functions (Figure 1.2). It carries out normative and operational functions relating to international drugs, crime and terrorism. Thus, its knowledge processing requirements demands diverse information architectures. For example, for operational functions like building capacity to fight against illegal drug production/use, crime and terrorism in a particular country, depends on self-reporting of the country in question, other-reporting from other countries (including intelligence and law enforcement agencies) to verify self reports, and problem reporting of the situation by the organizations policy making bodies.

Analyses of reports for normative functions are used to evaluate the impact of member countries activities on the goal of the organization, and to organize new conventions and agreements. Analyses for operational functions are useful in assessing each individual countries requirement (upon request of the country) to meet certain international agreements. Complex information systems that can be used to connect people together as well as connect people to documents, improve transparency of the organizations functions, and are useful in providing better quality analysis of the drugs and crime environment.

A categorization of technologies used by international organizations, based on Skyrme and Amidon [74], including non digital technologies like paper, used for KM is abstracted and summarized in Figure 3.6 below.

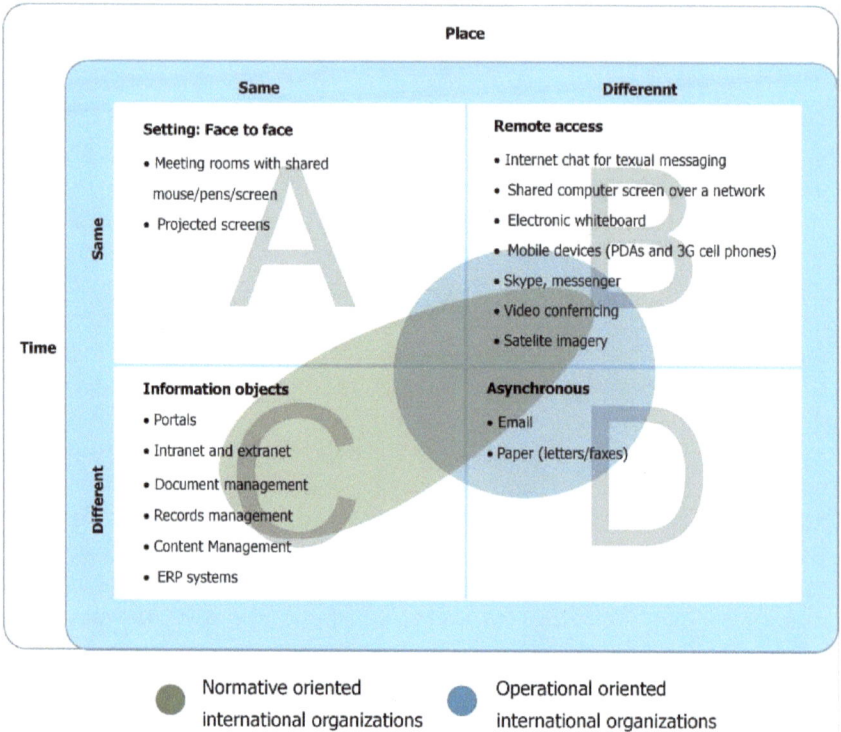

Figure 3.6: Categorization of technologies

(adapted from [74])

CHAPTER 4
THE PROCESS OF
MANAGING KNOWLEDGE

The knowledge chain model developed by Holsapple and Singh[143, 144], presents a model, analogous to Porter's value chain [145] that characterizes KM activities an organization can focus on to achieve better performance and competitiveness. This section extends this knowledge chain model (cf. Table 4.1) by applying it to international organizations functions (cf. Figure 4.1).

Table 4.1: Primary activities in the knowledge chain
(Source: [143])

	Definition
Knowledge acquisition	Acquiring knowledge from external sources and making it suitable for subsequent use
Knowledge selection	Selecting needed knowledge from internal sources and making it suitable for subsequent use
Knowledge generation	Producing knowledge by either discovery or derivation from existing knowledge

Knowledge assimilation	Altering the state of an organization's knowledge resources by distributing and storing acquired, selected, or generated knowledge
Knowledge Emission	Embedding knowledge into organizational outputs for release into the environment

The knowledge chain below (Figure 4.1) depicts the knowledge processing activities involved in both roles (normative and operational), embedded with the outcomes as the key performance indicators (KPIs) at each stage of the knowledge chain, including increased collaboration, increased information access, international recognition, and increased awareness of the challenges of managing knowledge (cf. Figure 2.25, Figure 2.24 and Appendix A for definitions of concepts). The KPIs are sorted from left to right in the order of importance below the knowledge chain activity (Figure 4.1). For example, "acquiring" the relevant expertise to implement parts of projects, hinges on successful collaboration among the stakeholders involved, followed by a recognition of the most qualified person(s) to do the job (if the expert(s) is a national of the country), as well as information access (using information technologies--IT) to an international expert database—in case no national experts are identified—that the project manager can pool from to assist in the project implementation.

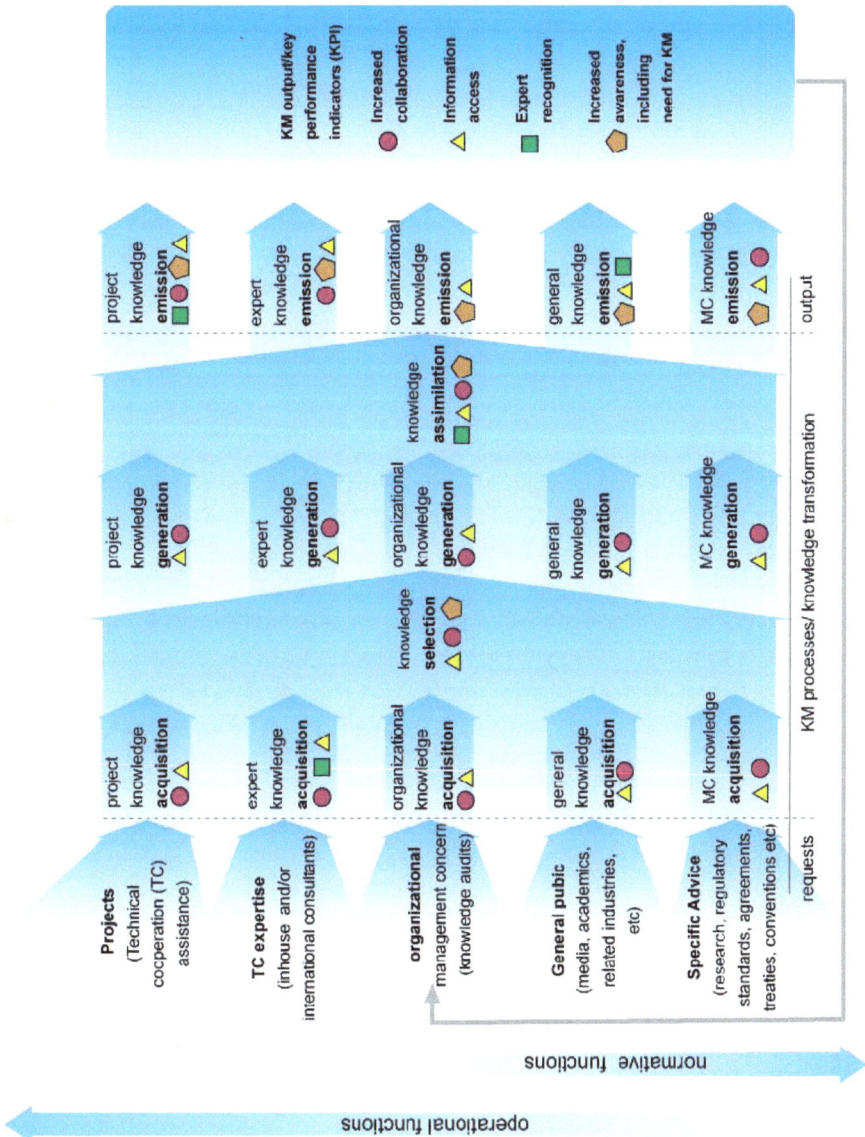

Figure 4.1: Knowledge chain for international organizations

4.1 KNOWLEDGE MANAGEMENT ACTIVITIES

Organizations in the sample (cf. Chapter 2) tended to focus their efforts differently, based on the functional orientation as shown below (Figure 4.2). For example, the IAEA's KM efforts were focused on organizing and preserving nuclear knowledge (cf. Section 2.1); and in UNIDO, an operational-oriented organization, the KM efforts were focused on knowledge sharing, and how to ensure that there is adequate feedback from the projects implemented in the field (member countries) into future projects (cf. Section 2.6).

A two dimensional matrix that describes the flow of the knowledge chain activities derived from the axial coding tables (Appendix B)— actions interactions column, against four primary knowledge management challenges [146] is shown below (Figure 4.2). Normative oriented organizations (cf. Section 1.2.3) focused their knowledge processing activities on problems (Figure 4.2, quadrant 1) within a specific domain. The newly-developed, (but currently piloted), Integrated Energy Information System (IEIS) in OPEC (also referred to as the "chart bank"), is used to reduce complexity, by presenting complex oil market information in graphical form, within the organization's portal, enabling staff and member country officials to "know what the organization knows" (Figure 4.2, quadrant 1), thereby making better use of the knowledge assets stored in databases. In operational organizations a focus is on solving novel problems. For example, the OSCE, an operational-oriented organization, is mandated with a wide range of tasks in Kosovo [147]: from institution building and democracy-building to promoting human rights and the rule of law. Knowledge generation (Figure 4.2, quadrant 2) and innovation are keys to remaining relevant to the stakeholders of operational-oriented organizations.

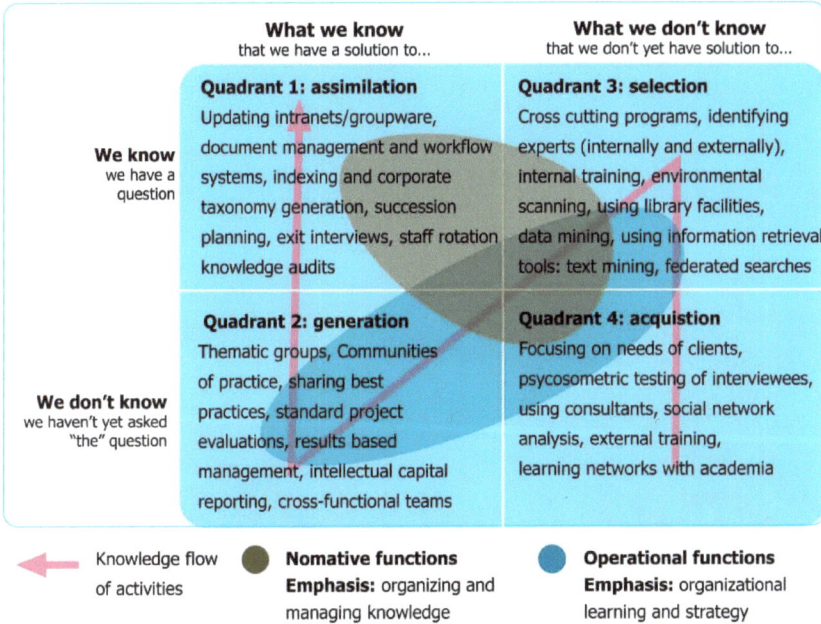

	What we know that we have a solution to...	**What we don't know** that we don't yet have solution to...
We know we have a question	**Quadrant 1: assimilation** Updating intranets/groupware, document management and workflow systems, indexing and corporate taxonomy generation, succession planning, exit interviews, staff rotation knowledge audits	**Quadrant 3: selection** Cross cutting programs, identifying experts (internally and externally), internal training, environmental scanning, using library facilities, data mining, using information retrieval tools: text mining, federated searches
We don't know we haven't yet asked "the" question	**Quadrant 2: generation** Thematic groups, Communities of practice, sharing best practices, standard project evaluations, results based management, intellectual capital reporting, cross-functional teams	**Quadrant 4: acquistion** Focusing on needs of clients, psycosometric testing of interviewees, using consultants, social network analysis, external training, learning networks with academia

Knowledge flow of activities

Nomative functions
Emphasis: organizing and managing knowledge

Operational functions
Emphasis: organizational learning and strategy

Figure 4.2: Strategic KM tools for international organizations

4.2 STAKEHOLDER POWER

According to Winstanley et al [31], stakeholders influence an organization by exercising power in different ways. In international organizations, these ways can be redefined as:

1. *Normative power:* the power to define the norms, rules, and **decision-making** procedures around which actors expectations converge in a given area of international relations [148].
2. *Operational power*: the power to determine how knowledge products and services (cf. Figure 3.4), offered by the organization are provided, by **allocation of resources**.

These two dimensions can be combined into a matrix, represented by Figure 4.3 and Figure 4.4. The matrices plot the stakeholder groups into four quadrants, and depict their dynamic interactions.

Member countries in quadrant A (cf. Figure 4.3 and Figure 4.4) have significant indirect power to drive KM in international organizations from the outside. As a result, these stakeholders can limit or determine KM initiatives through the amount of power they delegate to the organization.

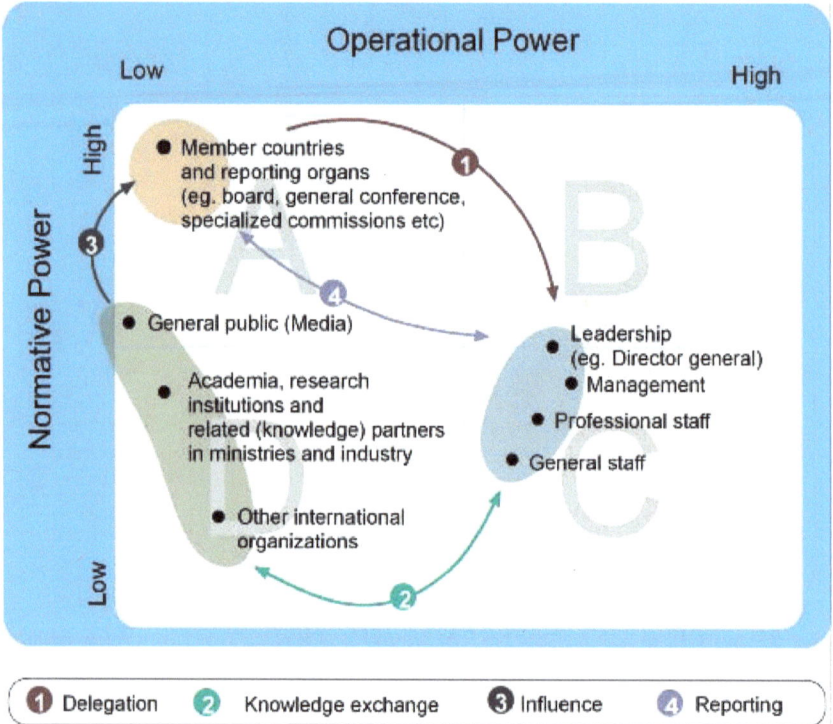

Figure 4.3: Stakeholder power matrix for normative functions

The idea that no single entity wields comprehensive power—high normative and operational power (cf. Figure 4.3: quadrant b and Figure 4.4: quadrant b) is validated in international relations theories on *anarchy* [149]—that is, there is no universal sovereign or worldwide government that can solely carry out functions "like resolving disputes or ordering the system"[4].

---

4 "Anarchy" in political science does not necessarily mean chaos or conflict or a world in disorder. It simply reflects the order of the international system: independent states with no central authority [149]   Mearsheimer, John. *The tragedy of great power politics.* New York: W. W. Norton & Company, 2001.

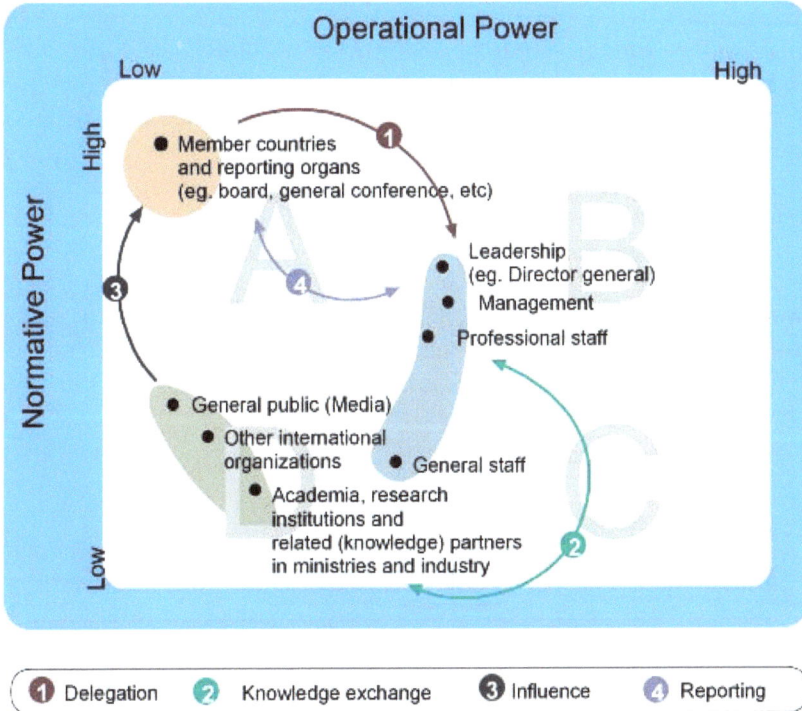

Figure 4.4: Stakeholder power matrix for operational functions

Member countries in quadrant A (Figure 4.4), however, delegate less operational power for operational functions (cf. Figure 4.4) and less normative power for normative functions (cf. Figure 4.3). Donor countries in UNIDO earmark their contributions towards industrial development, effectively limiting the scope of operational functions. For normative functions, member countries are obliged, as terms of membership, to contribute regularly, but they define among themselves normative policies. In OPEC, normative policy decisions affecting production levels are decided by the Member Country representatives and not by the organization's management.

General public in quadrant A (Figure 4.3) have more normative power for normative functions (cf. Figure 4.4). This stems from the idea that for normative functions to be successful, a variety of actors are required (cf. Section 3.1) [14], which includes the general public (media). For example, in the EU, the constitution was rejected by EU citizens (Section 2.8).

Communities of interest (academia, general public, government ministry [knowledge workers] and related industries) in quadrant D (Figure 4.3 and Figure 4.4) have low normative and operational power—normally relegated to workshops, conferences and seminars. The effectiveness (or ineffectiveness) of such interactions contributes to the levels of influence these communities exert on governments in issue areas, and, consequently, can form (or hinder) new normative functions by member countries. The lack of data transparency in the oil markets in the 1990s lead market analysts to speculate about market fundamentals (cf. Section 2.4), resulting in sharp increases in the oil prices during this period. Thus exchange of information and data with communities of interest to OPEC, such as through the Joint Oil Data Initiative (JODI), contribute towards stabilizing the oil market (cf. Section 2.4) [150].

4.3 CLASSIFYING EXPLICIT KNOWLEDGE FOR TRANSPARENCY

Transparency is crucial for the effectiveness of international organizations [124]. The processes of the knowledge chain (cf. Figure 4.1), including the acquisition, analysis and dissemination of regular prompt and accurate information, underpins the one of the most important functions of international organizations. All organizations in the sample are making efforts to automate and codify their administrative and substantive work, using ERP, document management, records management systems and so on. Information systems enables activities of international organizations to mobilize resources on time, including staff, equipment, setting up offices, ensuring logistic support, to transfer resources from one operation to the next and to account for funds and in-kind contributions that make up parts of its administrative and substantive activities.

In order to enhance the transparency of information assets, a logical classification of information is necessary [151]. Functions and activities of international organizations provide a stable framework for classifying information than organizational structures [152]. In UNIDO, the organizational structure has changed 24 times since 1985 [153]—but its basic focus on operational matters of international significance, related to industrial development, remains the same. Therefore, a function-based approach can anchor information firmly in the processes of international organizations. A functions-based classification of information has the following advantages, as it helps international organizations to:

- Identify records that should be created because of their evidential value for the member countries;
- Recognize high priority records that should be captured because of their significance to member countries;
- Make decisions on retention; and
- Sentence records at the point of creation [154]

Building upon the accumulated knowledge of international organizations' functions (**operational** functions are centred on technical cooperation work and **normative** functions are centred on research, norms and standards) and its knowledge chain (cf. Section Chapter 4) and knowledge products (cf. Section Figure 3.4), a generic classification scheme (BCS) can be developed, a hierarchical model of the relationships between an organizations functions, activities and transactions [155] as shown in Figure 4.5 below.

The analytical process for creating a BCS (cf. Figure 4.5) starts with a "big picture" view of the organizations activity and breaks it down to more detailed parts [155]. The component parts are broken down in descending order as the organizations functions, activities and transactions.

Operational functions (cf. Figure 4.5) in a BCS can be used to group everything related to field work i.e. technical cooperation activities, from project schedules and project files to lessons learned, project assessments and so on. The normative function category in the BCS can be used to group all activities relating to the organizations multilateral networks with other actors in international affairs (such as information on outcomes of meetings with other international organizations and governments), as well as public information, like public websites, publications and public records. Management functions can be used to group the secretariat and administrative aspects, such as human resources management and finance information.

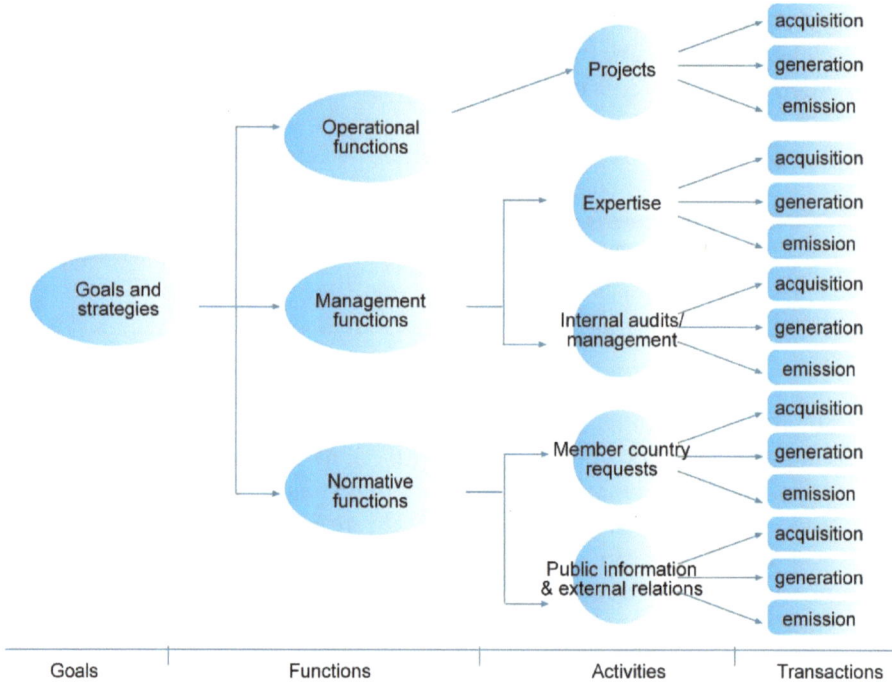

Figure 4.5: Analysis of business activity for a BCS

Although the analysis above, derived from a hierarchical depiction of a generic functions and activities of international organizations (cf. Figure 4.5) , can be used as a starting point for designing a BCS, the scale of these components is relative, rather than absolute. For example, business transactions are relative in scale to organizations. Transaction in an international organization include information coming in (acquisition), solutions being generated to meet these requests, taking into consideration prior knowledge (generation), and information going out to various stakeholders (emission) (cf. Section Chapter 4). In all cases, the scale of transactional components will need to be manipulated to create a meaningful practical business classification scheme for a particular organization, taking into consideration other aspects of information management, like metadata, taxonomies, ontologies, security requirements (cf. Section 3.1.2), and so on.

4.4 RECOMMENDATIONS

Becoming knowledge focused in international organizations involves a broad scope, where a large variety of latent explicit and implicit factors are involved (cf. Section Chapter 3), including collaboration, capacity building and stakeholder behaviour, involving trust, politics, stakeholder interactions and leadership, as well as the reflective consideration of the knowledge chain processes (cf. Figure 4.1). Different internal and external pressures led organizations to manage their knowledge, varying from organization to organization (cf. Section Chapter 2), and accordingly were interpreted differently, based on their functional mandate. However among all these concepts and ideas, there is a generic process of **strategic analysis, strategic choice and strategic implementation** which can be applied [156]. This section recommends 12 iterative steps involved in this generic process, based on the findings in this research.

STRATEGIC ANALYSIS

Step 1: Determine the functional orientation of the organization in terms of normative/operational classification described in Section 1.2 and Section 1.3. Normative functions, depend more on established research knowledge (embedded knowledge), intended to influence the perceptions of international actors within a specified set of issues. Operational functions require direct contributions of key technical specialists (embodied knowledge), communications and collaboration with stakeholders (encultured knowledge), and the creative ability of experts (embrained knowledge), used for sharing the problem of implementing policy decisions.

Step 2: Analyze the key external and internal pressures facing organizations in terms of the categories identified for the KM drivers (cf. Section 2.9 and Appendix A for definitions of categories)—which are based on the functional orientation.

Step 3: Identify intellectual capital resources and strategic capabilities that the organization has to meet in the internal and external pressures (cf. Figure 1.3).

Step 4: Identify particular knowledge products, including project management expertise types and advice types required to meet the mandate of the organization (cf. Figure 3.4)

STRATEGIC CHOICE OF TOOLS

Step 5: Evaluate and select strategic knowledge management tools and options for addressing various knowledge problems (cf. Figure 4.2) in the knowledge chain process.

STRATEGIC IMPLEMENTATION OF KM

Step 6: Restructure internal knowledge processes according to the knowledge chain (cf. Figure 4.1). For example, thematic groups and communities of practices can be formed around the knowledge chain, delegating responsibility (to groups/individuals) for knowledge products (cf. Figure 3.4) at each stage of the knowledge chain. Inherent in this step is the need for good communication skills. Formal training and workshops on *interpersonal communication skills* in an intercultural environment can increase productivity and reduce misunderstanding in this step.

Step 7: Explicit knowledge can be classified according to the main functions and activities of the organization (cf. Section 4.3), as a first step in the creation of a business classification scheme [155], and other more detailed classifications like taxonomies, thesauruses, semantic networks, ontologies and so on [157], that are useful for structuring electronic information and documents. Inherent in this step is the need for highly skilled information architects, which are able to classify and organize information assets for better user experience.

Step 8: Implement appropriate technologies, based on the orientation of the organization (cf. Section 3.3). Due to the types of knowledge inherent in the organizations functions (cf. Step 1): normatively oriented organizations should focus technology implementation on connecting communities (and individuals) to explicit knowledge objects, particularly useful for research, as well as public information. For example, using documents management systems and multimedia, podcasts, portals and so on normative organizations can more proactively reach diverse interested actors in the public and academia. Operationally oriented organizations, on the other hand, should focus on using technology to connect community leaders together, aiding decision making processes. For example, using tools like skype (for phone calls and integrated messaging), white boards, web-based project and resource management tools, video conferencing, as well as other social networking tools (cf. Figure 3.5). Operational functions, including technical assistance projects, can be carried out more expeditiously, when decision makers are empowered with technology to communicate with the right experts at the right time—even across many distances and time zones.

Step 9: Manage the culture change, keeping in mind the explicit and more particularly implicit factors involved in knowledge management in international organizations, such as stakeholder power relations (cf. Section 4.2) and trust building interactions (using game theory models [158]) (cf. Section 3.1) that can affect stakeholder behaviour, collaboration and capacity building.

Step 10: Overlap retiring staff with new staff, particularly for operational functions—due to the complexity of types of knowledge inherent in operational functions (cf. step 1).

Step 11: Conduct exit interviews for staff that are leaving—in the presence of new (incoming) staff members assuming the same roles (cf. Step 10), in order to transfer knowledge to incoming staff members.

Step 12: Conduct regular knowledge audits (at different stages of the knowledge chain) to ensure that knowledge is integrated vertically and horizontally within the organization—from management to professional and general staff cross departmentally. Knowledge audits should include the use of intellectual capital methods like the Holistic Value Approach (HVA)[159] to measure the impact of the intellectual capital resources on the key performance indicators of the knowledge chain (cf. Figure 4.1 and Figure 5.1), as well as to report progress (that is results-based) to member countries and the general public.

This step implies a new management role—that is to say international organizations need knowledge managers that can assess knowledge flows within the organization, working with other senior managers, giving strategic advice on how to improve the status quo within and beyond the organizations boundaries from a knowledge process perspective.

CHAPTER 5
CONCLUSIONS

KM research has rarely studied the strategy of becoming knowledge focused in international organizations, especially from the viewpoint of the organizations themselves. Such research has confined itself to identification and measurement of adaptation [42] or "maladaptation" of KM theory [41], to international organizations, without first understanding the idiosyncratic drivers for KM in the organizations themselves.

The theoretical frameworks that have been employed in an attempt to explain the experience of becoming knowledge focused in international organizations, particularly the view that managing knowledge is simply about generation, codifying and transfer of explicit knowledge (cf. Section 1.3.1), have proved inadequate in accounting for the richer experience that such organizations encounter (cf. Section Chapter 4).

Paradoxically, literature on KM relates more closely to the experience described by those professional and management staff charged with managing knowledge in international organizations. These organizations were found to undergo a profound reconstruction of purpose, driven in part by external stakeholders, before the need for KM became apparent. KM affects an international organization differently based on its functions, including how it manages intellectual capital—not as a reactive, but as a reflective activity. This research has provided insight into the challenges faced by international organizations as they attempt to become more knowledge focused, and has outlined an integrated framework (cf. Section **4.4**) that can be used as potential strategies that will assist the process of becoming knowledge focused.

This book has attempted a cross-disciplinary synthesis by extending existing KM research with insight from international organizations' functions. It has demonstrated how applying a modified grounded theory can lead to the emergence of a theoretical framework that can predict the way international organizations are likely to respond to pressures from member countries by becoming more knowledge focused. This framework was applied both to normative oriented organizations such as the European Union (EU), the International Atomic Energy Agency (IAEA), the International Maritime Organization (IMO), the Organization of the Petroleum Exporting Countries (OPEC), the United Nations Office on Drugs and Crime (UNODC), and to operationally oriented organizations such as the OPEC Fund for International Development (OFID), the Organization for Security and Co-operation in Europe (OSCE), the United Nations Industrial Development Organization (UNIDO) which all faced different types of pressures (cf. Section Chapter 2). Initiatives can be developed on the basis of this research to guide knowledge managers to the primary concerns of international organizations and their stakeholders and where KM may be of the greatest benefit (cf. Section **4.4**).

Increasing the understanding of problems faced by international organizations highlights what kinds of KM activities, strategies and performance indicators are likely to be most effective. An example of this is the demonstrable importance of managing stakeholder behaviour in response to changing geopolitical realities. For this to happen effectively, top management must be involved from the start to focus the organization on its core competencies and experiences and strengthen collaborative action and partnerships in dealing with multifaceted international affairs. Promoting desirable behaviour, such as knowledge-sharing, requires leadership and inspiration—particularly from the Director General or equivalent - as well as management sensitivity to factors motivating stakeholders in international organizations. The analysis also shows that preoccupation with individual work or IT alone, rather than organizational dynamics, including explicit and implicit factors such as collaboration, capacity building and stakeholder behaviour, involving trust, politics, stakeholder interactions and leadership, as well as the reflective consideration of the business functions, business classification schemes, knowledge products, and knowledge chain processes [160], prevents full comprehension of the organization's problems and limits the assistance that can be provided by knowledge managers to make the organization better at managing its knowledge.

5.1 FUTURE RESEARCH

The theoretical frameworks developed in this research do not provide methods that can be used to accurately assess an international organizations progress towards becoming knowledge focused. To be effective, it will therefore be necessary to develop instrumental frameworks to measure how well the theory developed in this work has been applied. For example, it will be beneficial to incorporate other explanatory perspectives in order to develop a theoretical model for strategically measuring performance of international organizations in terms of knowledge. Such a model can provide a basis for more proactively managing the value of intellectual capital against key performance indicators of the knowledge chain (cf. Figure 5.1), using intellectual capital methods like the Holistic Value Approach (HVA)[159].

A tool kit for measuring the value/impact of performance indicators of the knowledge chain (cf. Figure 4.1) of international organizations can be developed, by building upon accumulated knowledge of international organizations' functions (**operational** activities are centred on technical cooperation work and **normative** activities are centred on research, norms and standards), as well as research into intellectual capital resources (cf. Figure 1.3), and intellectual capital methods. An illustration of such a research direction is shown in Figure 5.1 below.

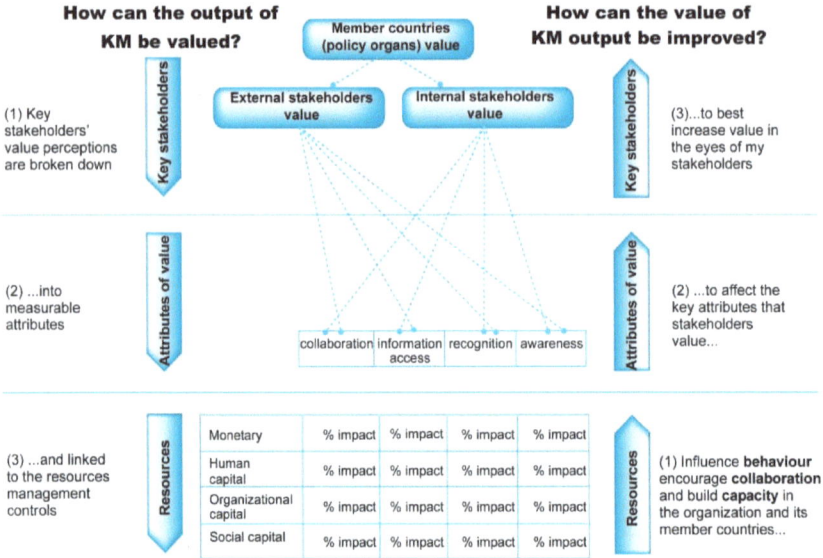

Figure 5.1: knowledge focused value management in international organizations

5.2 BECOMING KNOWLEDGE FOCUSED

Few researchers like myself will admit that while there is really nothing new about managing knowledge [5, 58]—all organizations do it, albeit reactively - paradoxically, there is something new about it when done reflectively, and as an outcome of strategy—it positively transforms organizations, by increasing awareness of the challenges of improving staff and organizational effectiveness and efficiency (cf. Figure 5.2 below)

KM efficiency:
Activities where collaboration is actively encouraged, stakeholder capacity is assessed and strengthened, and stakeholder behaviour is strategically managed within the knowledge chain.

'[KM issue]'

'we have to get better at KM'

KM inefficiency:
Activities without strategically encouraging collaboration, building capacity and managing behaviour.

Becoming Knowledge Focused
The term "Becoming knowledge focused" describes the progression from a state of KM inefficiency to becoming more efficient at KM. The paradigm shift was a conscious appreciation of the impact of knowledge and the need to manage it as the vital resource of the organization.

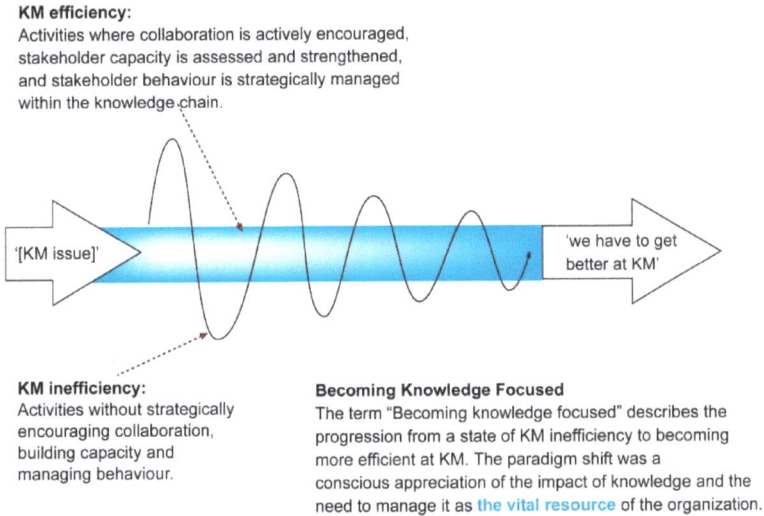

Figure 5.2: KM as a process of becoming knowledge focused

The difference lies in the appreciation of the critical importance of the intangibles of human knowledge to the survival of an organization [161]. It is this focused view of the international organization as primarily a knowledge broker and custodian of international norms and standards, as well as a knowledge service provider through normative and operational functions that marks the fundamental difference in becoming knowledge focused in international organizations. In this sense, KM is not new to international organizations, but becoming knowledge focused is. It is characterized by an acute awareness of the challenges of managing stakeholder behaviour, collaboration and building upon skills and experiences.

According to the knowledge-based view of the firm from literature such as Rumelt [162], Wernerfelt [163], Dierickx [164], Barney [165], Hall [166], the main emphasis of knowledge management on building and managing a reflective capacity to know and derive value from such knowledge, and to offer a process perspective on how to improve work. The knowledge-based view of international organizations, developed in the research, can provide a process perspective by complementing conventional approaches to an international organization's functions. It is from this perspective that this research can be translated and understood by other international organizations to leverage their organizational strategies.

As international relations have evolved, following the break-up of the Soviet Union [13, 167], one of the primary purposes of international organizations is to serve their member countries—towards achieving the Millennium Development Goals (MDG) [88] set out in United Nations Millennium Declaration (MD), adopted by world leaders. It is from this perspective of renewed multilateral cooperation, the basis for organizing and governing internationally, that becoming knowledge focused is apparent as a way forward. Therefore becoming knowledge focused in international organizations is about developing reflective practices for effectively harnessing the world's political, scientific, and technological knowledge in the 21th century, to attain the ideals of human dignity, freedom, democracy, peace and development for all through international organizations functions.

Acronyms

AFDB THE AFRICAN DEVELOPMENT BANK

ADB THE ASIAN DEVELOPMENT BANK

BCS BUSINESS CLASSIFICATION SCHEME

CEB CHIEF EXECUTIVE BOARD OF THE UNITED
NATIONS SYSTEM

DM DOCUMENTS MANAGEMENT

DOD DEPARTMENT OF DEFENSE, USA

EDM ENTERPRISE DOCUMENT MANAGEMENT

EBRD THE EUROPEAN BANK FOR RECONSTRUCTION
AND DEVELOPMENT

ERP ENTERPRISE RESOURCE PLANNING SYSTEMS

EU EUROPEAN UNION

FAO FOOD AND AGRICULTURE ORGANIZATION

GA GENERAL ASSEMBLY

GEF GLOBAL ENVIRONMENT FACILITY

GISIS   GLOBAL INTEGRATED SHIPPING INFORMATION
        SYSTEM

GT   GROUNDED THEORY

HIPC   HEAVILY INDEBTED POOR COUNTRIES

IAEA   INTERNATIONAL ATOMIC ENERGY AGENCY

IC   INTELLECTUAL CAPITAL

IDB   INTER-AMERICAN DEVELOPMENT BANK

IFAD   INTERNATIONAL FUND FOR AGRICULTURAL
       DEVELOPMENT

IMO   INTERNATIONAL MARITIME ORGANIZATION

INIS   INTERNATIONAL NUCLEAR INFORMATION
       SYSTEM

IRMA   INTEGRATED RESOURCE MANAGEMENT SYSTEM

IT   INFORMATION TECHNOLOGY

KIF   KNOWLEDGE INTENSIVE FIRM

KM   KNOWLEDGE MANAGEMENT

KMS   KNOWLEDGE MANAGEMENT SYSTEMS

KS KNOWLEDGE SHARING

NKM NUCLEAR KNOWLEDGE MANAGEMENT

NOC NATIONAL OIL COMPANY

LCD LEAST DEVELOPED COUNTRIES

MARPOL INTERNATIONAL CONVENTION FOR THE PREVENTION OF POLLUTION FROM SHIPS [168]

MDG MILLENIUM DEVELOPMENT GOALS

OSCE ORGANIZATION FOR SECURITY AND CO-OPERATION IN EUROPE

OPEC ORGANIZATION OF THE PETROLEUM EXPORTING COUNTRIES

OFID OPEC FUND FOR INTERNATIONAL DEVELOPMENT

RM RECORDS MANAGEMENT

UN UNITED NATIONS

UNDP UNITED NATIONS DEVELOPMENT PROGRAM

UNFIP UNITED NATIONS FUND FOR INTERNATIONAL PARTNERSHIPS

UNFPA   UNITED NATIONS POPULATION FUND

UNHCR   UNITED NATIONS HIGH COMMISSIONER FOR
        REFUGEES.

UNICEF UNITED NATIONS CHILDREN'S FUND

UNIDO   UNITED NATIONS INDUSTRIAL DEVELOPMENT
        ORGANIZATION

UNODC   UNITED NATIONS OFFICE ON DRUGS AND
        CRIME

WFP   WORLD FOOD PROGRAM

WHO   WORLD HEALTH ORGANIZATION

WMD   WEAPONS OF MASS DESTRUCTION

WTO   WORLD TRADE ORGANIZATION

WWII   SECOND WORLD WAR

APPENDIX A

No.	Category	Definition
1	Age pyramid	The age profile of employees eligible to retire in the short to medium term (between 5 and 10 years).
2	Attrition	A reduction in the number of skilled people in a particular field or region, as through retirement or resignation
3	Awareness	**Political**: The increased general understanding of the normative positions, and efforts of an organization and its member countries. **KM awareness**: The initial stage of the process of learning about the limits of the organization's ongoing strategic efforts.
4	Capacity building	The commitment to the development of sustainable skills, resources, infrastructure, and institutions that can improve the lives of people in developing countries and countries in (economic, political and social) transition.
5	Collaboration	**Formal**: Adjusting to greater numbers and greater diversity of actors at the macro level, in order to ensure support for new normative functions. This requires universal participation and formal equality among all participants. **Informal**: The act of specialists working together at the micro level, within and beyond the organization's boundaries.
6	Competency upgrade	The need to increase the capability of individual staff, and the organization as a whole to perform adequately the mandate of the organization.

7	Competition	Simultaneous demand, by two or more international organizations' programs and related institutions, for limited resources from established funds and programs (such as UNDP, GEF and so on) or directly from donor countries.
8	Geopolitics	The combination of geographic and political factors relating to or influencing an international organization
9	Information access	Managed access to information objects and applications
10	Mandate overlap	The internal and external duplication of obligation across two or more international organizations.
11	Perceptions	**Public:** Those subjective judgements of the general public that result from any significant event related to an international organization. **Political:** The political position of governments with regards to the mandate of an international organization
12	Recognition	**Organizational:** The favourable attention for the organizations achievements **Expertise:** Acknowledgement of individual (or a group) contribution towards a collective goal.
13	Recruitment	The challenge of attracting and retaining talent.
14	Reform	**Programmatic:** changes proposed (or implemented), at the governing sphere, due to demands of member countries and constituents relating to "how" programs are implemented. **Administrative:** changes implemented by management at the organizational level.
15	Reporting structures	The fixed hierarchical procedures for reporting among numerous offices/organs of an organization.

16	Safety	The concern for unintended injury or risk due to behaviour (e.g. the environment)
17	Security	Any threat to international peace and economic stability.
18	Succession	Need for preparing suitable strategies to ensure continuity of workforce at the organizational and/or global level.

APPENDIX B

GROUNDED THEORY

The grounded theory methodology as described by Strauss and Corbin [94, 169], using interviews and document studies for data collection, combined with findings from literature, helped identify processes involved in managing knowledge in international organizations. The KM processes discovered suggests that managing knowledge in international organizations is a complex cyclical activity that leads an international organization to become more knowledge focused.

AXIAL CODING

Axial coding is a term Strauss [94] used to describe the phase in the analysis where concepts revolve around a category or "axis", linking other categories and dimensions with a particular category. To simplify this process, rather than look at all kinds of relations, emphasis was placed on causal relationships, facilitating the emergence of cumulative knowledge about relationships between particular categories and other categories and sub-categories.

Two interrelated knowledge management contexts were evident in all the organizations: the concerns of the external stakeholders and those of the internal stakeholders (cf. Exhibit 1 to Exhibit 15). The external context (at the macro level) revolved around particular concerns of the organizations' external stakeholders--especially the organizations' member countries. For example, issues related to geopolitics, political/public perceptions, security and safety issues were the main concern of the external stakeholders of the IAEA, UNODC, OPEC, and so on (cf. Exhibit 1 to Exhibit 15), and issues related to age pyramid, recruitment, succession planning, and so on, were important to the internal stakeholders in these organizations.

Positive outcomes, such as: better "information access" for stakeholders, "recognition" of the organizations' leadership on particular issues of global significance and a greater "awareness" among the organizations' stakeholders of the position of their respective organizations, and so on resulted from the organizations' focus on managing knowledge within and beyond their boundaries.

For example, in the IAEA, the external concerns (at the macro level) revolved around "attrition" (cf. Section 2.1) of specialists in the nuclear industry. The rapid attrition rate caused recruitment challenges for the organization, as there was a talent scarcity of qualified people. Becoming knowledge focused in the IAEA resulted in an increased awareness (cf. Section 2.1) of the need for workforce planning at the macro level and knowledge management within the organization.

The paradigm model [94], presented in abbreviated form (cf. Exhibit 1 to Exhibit 15), revealed the relationships within the broad macro/micro classifications of external versus internal contexts by describing, (a) the causal conditions, (b) the context, (c) the intervening conditions that assisted or hindered the KM actions or interactions taken and, (e) the consequences of the actions and interactions taken. The use of the paradigm model helped relationships between the categories to emerge.

CONTEXT: Agency starts to manage knowledge within the organization to offset potential skills loss, amid age pyramid		
Casual conditions	**Actions/interactions**	**Consequences**
● ageing and retirement of skilled management and professional staff **AGE PYRAMID** ● talent scarcity ● statutory turnover ● lack of budget for staff overlap ● gaps in filling vacancies ● gaps in project overlap **RECRUITMENT** ● vertical/bureaucratic ● one man projects ● decentralized IT **REPORTING STRUCTURES** ● management concern with ensuring that organizational memory is not lost when staff leave organization **SUCCESSION**	● creating "one house" concept ● looking at cross cutting programs ● recognizing teamwork (awards) ● using psychometric tests to screen recruits at leadership levels ● recruiting "team players" at leadership levels ● exit interviews (KM & HR) ● youth programs ● developing portal (Nucleus) ● managing content (OpenText) ● investigating enterprise resource planning solutions (ERP) ● virtualizing teamwork ● forming task force on KM ● employing knowledge managers ● creating the DG briefs ● matrix management ● results based management	● support from member countries ● increased management interest of need for internal knowledge management ● intensifying/formalizing KM **AWARENESS**

(Left vertical label: **CAPACITY BUILDING**)

(Right vertical label: **INDIVIDUAL STAKEHOLDER BEHAVIOR**)

COLLABORATION

Exhibit 1: Illustration of axial coding for internal context in the IAEA

CONTEXT: amid increasing international recognition for IAEA,
there is increasing loss of technical competencies in nuclear field worldwide

Casual conditions	Actions/interactions	Consequences
● aging management in industry ● government deregulation ● high attrition rate in industry **ATTRITION** ● increasing risk to operations of reactors ● increasing risk of radioactive waste mismanagement ● safe decommissioning & decontamination issues **SAFETY** ● prospects for nuclear power ● negative public perceptions of industry ● decreasing academic interest in nuclear sciences ● negative perception of job prospects in industry **PERCEPTIONS** ● end of the cold war ● decreasing incentive for stocking nuclear weapons and impact on nuclear proliferation ● Threat of international terrorism **GEOPOLITICS** ● safeguarding aquisition and use of nuclear energy **SECURITY**	● revamping INIS database (International Nuclear Information System) to include Computer Assisted Indexing (CAI) ● participating in WANO (World Association of Nuclear Operators) ● starting the knowledge preservation project (technical cooperation) ● organizing conference on NKM ● networking with academic institutions (e.g. World Nuclear University) ● introductory course on agency safeguards (ICAS) ● active learning, mentoring and on the job training (safeguards) ● planning for continuity of knowledge in safeguards ● increased tenure for inspectors ● changing procedures and role of inspectors (assuming consultancy roles) ● changes in inspector equipment and technology (e.g. satellite technologies)	● increased access and use of INIS database worldwide **INFORMATION ACCESS** ● recognition of work--Nobel Prize **RECOGNITION** ● increased industry awareness of need for NKM **AWARENESS** ● increased nuclear industry stakeholder collaboration towards nuclear knowledge management ● recognizing strength of cultural diversity and method of approach **COLLABORATION**

(left margin, vertical) **CAPACITY BUILDING**

(right margin, vertical) **INDIVIDUAL STAKEHOLDER BEHAVIOR**

COLLABORATION

Exhibit 2: Illustration of axial coding for external context in the IAEA

CONTEXT: IMO embarks on change management with a focus on improving information exchange and knowledge sharing		
Casual conditions	**Actions/interactions**	**Consequences**
● ageing and retirement of skilled management and professional staff (75% of workforce over 50) **AGE PYRAMID** ● talent scarcity ● gaps in filling vacancies **RECRUITMENT** ● vertical/bureaucratic ● lack of delegation ● lack of oversight and decision support ● too many content administrators that input data from manually (date sent from MCs) ● lack of transparency in processes ● inefficiencies: plenty of non core business resources and manpower **REPORTING STRUCTURES** ● management concern with ensuring that organizational memory is not lost when staff leave organization **SUCCESSION**	● consolidating desperate systems and databases (security, cost state control, piracy, standards on carrying dangerous goods etc. all related to ships) into GISIS portal ● provide MCs with a view where they can enter info from source (GISIS--used to implement mandate portal). ● hiring business consultants like Mannet and Deloitte & Touche to recommend review and recommend changes to processes, budgets and expenditure ● implementing ERP solutions: procurement, ERM, CRM, business warehouse, core financials) ● administrator of the GISIS in every country (approximately 2000 administrators in total); system hosted in IMO ● bulletin board exchange of ideas (one to many) supplements face to face ● virtualizing teamwork (MC use stems to enter data) ● creating the DG briefs ● matrix management	● support from member countries ● increased management interest of need for internal knowledge management **AWARENESS** ● 30 administrators users looking after many parts of the data (secretaries to committee) ● automated systems: content admin now review input before committing into DB ● automating compliance from conventions for MCs (gathering data, reporting, sharing, real-time progress) for entire world shipping community ● 30,000 public users, 2000 admin county and secretariat staff ● info exchange from flag and port state (management stakeholders) ● technical exchange: (inspectors, standards) **INFORMATION ACCESS**

CAPACITY BUILDING

INDIVIDUAL STAKEHOLDER BEHAVIOR

COLLABORATION

Exhibit 3: Illustration of axial coding for internal context in the IMO

CONTEXT: Increasing regional and inter-governmental maritime agreements outside IMO's framework		
Casual conditions	**Actions/interactions**	**Consequences**
• government deregulation • high attrition rate in industry **ATTRITION** • increasing risk to the environment (oil pollution--Torrey Canyon disaster, Exxon Valdez disaster, the Erika disaster and the Prestige disaster) • Titanic and other passenger disasters • environmental treaties **SAFETY** • negative public perceptions of shipping industry • perception of IMO as slow to act. (EU introduced regional standards regarding single hall tankers) **PUBLIC PERCEPTIONS** • end of the cold war and increasing trade • sustainable development paradigm • shipping disasters: Exxon valdex, Estonia, Erika, Prestige • threat of international terrorism **GEOPOLITICS** • ensuring the uninterrupted international seaborne trade **SECURITY**	• seeking signatories to environmental treaties (e.g. Ballistic Water Management convention) • providing ubiquitous information systems (web portal access) for port and flat countries. • revamping GISIS database (Global integrated Ship Information system) • organizing conferences and conventions and technical assistance project s to better regulate shipping • prevention of pollution at sea convention (MARPOL) • safety of life at sea convention (SOLAS) • networking with academic institutions to implement the Standards of Training, Certification and Watchkeeping (STCW) convention. For example the world maritime university, IMO international maritime law institute, IMO international maritime academy, fellowships and trainning in IMO secretariat • workforce succession planning via the (via STCW) • changing procedures and design of oil tankers	• increased access and use of GISIS portal worldwide **INFORMATION ACCESS** • recognition of work of IMO **RECOGNITION** • increased industry awareness of need for international standards in shipping • increasing awareness of environmental impact of shipping **AWARENESS** • increased shipping industry stakeholder collaboration • recognizing need to reconcile diversity of laws regarding shipping **COLLABORATION**

CAPACITY BUILDING (left vertical label)

INDIVIDUAL STAKEHOLDER BEHAVIOR (right vertical label)

COLLABORATION

Exhibit 4: Illustration of axial coding for external context in the IMO

CONTEXT: management starts to implement workforce and succession plans to meet its expanding mandate

CAPACITY BUILDING

Casual conditions	Actions/interactions	Consequences
● retirement of skilled professionals **AGE PYRAMID** ● talent scarcity **RECRUITMENT** ● gaps in filling vacancies **SUCESSION** ● information sourcing for timely evaluation of projects ● pockets of practices **REPORTING STRUCTURES** ● management concern with upgrading human capital to increase its ability to deliver on its evolving mandate (private sector operations) **COMPETENCY UPGRADE**	● Disclosure of information on the website ● looking at cross cutting programs with other IFI to meet international expectations of MDG ● IFI development committee meeting (2x a year) ● quadrupling its human resources: recruiting very experienced professionals as managers from other IFIs and recruiting young professionals at lower levels to learn from and succeed staff ● youth programs (internships) ● deploying electronic records and documents management systems (OPEN text) ● moving from IBM mainframes in the 80s to PC and client server architecture ● developing quality criteria for benchmarking and classifying lessons learned	● increased access and use of network ● increased efficiency and timeliness of information dissemination (website) **INFORMATION ACCESS** ● increased collaboration with other IFIs and development agencies ● lean organization, with focused competencies ● recognizing strength of diversity and method of approach among international staff **COLLABORATION** ● increased organizational awareness of need for managing human capital ● awareness of need for succession planning ● increased awareness of the work of the organization (due to information disclosure on the website) **AWARENESS**

INDIVIDUAL STAKEHOLDER BEHAVIOR

COLLABORATION

Exhibit 5: Illustration of axial coding for internal context in OFID

	CONTEXT: the expansion of the organizations mandate to include the private sector		
CAPACITY BUILDING	**Casual conditions**	**Actions/interactions**	**Consequences**
	● end of cold war ● International agreements on MDG (2000 UN millennium summit) ● disappointing results the MDG (2002 World Summit on Sustainable Development) ● increasing liberalization and globalisation ● energy security ● debt relief (HIPC) ● global warming **GEOPOLITICS** ● Transparency in Bretton woods institutions and projects **COMPETITION** ● Demand outstrips capacity of all IFIs together **PERCEPTION** ● Increasing number of programs without clear programmatic focus (overlap with other IFIs) **MANDATE OVERLAP** ● pressure from member countries and recipient communities and governments for expansion of the OFID programs to include private sector operations **REFORM**	● seeking strategic partnerships with other IFIs and aid communities ● codification of OFIDs operational activities (planning and reporting, using ERP) ● developing the a new corporate identity ● Creating a new IT department to take advantage of information systems and improve information management. ● participating in the international conferences of major IFIs like the world bank and IMF ● channeling economic and environmental funds and services where they can have a "catalytic" role and lead to greater impact ● Articulating with the existing initiatives and efforts of communities and building on their strengths through "social projects" using world bank, the oldest IFI as template for protocols and procedures, enabling better transparency among implementing agencies	● strategic partnerships with other IFIs i.e. World Bank & IMF etc. on programs such as the MDG and HIPC. ● recognizing cultural diversity among recipient countries **COLLABORATION** ● increased access and use information systems **INFORMATION ACCESS** ● recognition for OFID by other IFIs and development agents **RECOGNITION** ● increased stakeholder awareness of need for better cooperation and synergy in international developmental finance in order to achieve the MDG by 2015 **AWARENESS**	**INDIVIDUAL STAKEHOLDER BEHAVIOR**
	COLLABORATION		

Exhibit 6: Illustration of axial coding for external context in OFID

CONTEXT: OPEC plans to strategically improve knowledge sharing and KM		
Casual conditions	**Actions/interactions**	**Consequences**
● ageing and retirement of skilled professional support staff in the organization **AGE PYRAMID** ● talent scarcity (in certain member countries well as in OECD and industry) ● statutory turnover ● lack of budget for staff overlap ● gaps in filling vacancies ● gaps in project overlap **RECRUITMENT** ● vertical/bureaucratic ● one man projects **REPORTING STRUCTURES** ● management concern with ensuring that organizational memory is not lost when staff leave organization ● increasing proliferation of paper documents **SUCCESSION**	● creating task forces and emphasis on teamwork ● looking at cross cutting programs ● proposing HR strategies for strengthening the secretariat ● focusing on organization structure to strategically strengthen the organization ● seeking technical assistance for MCs ● youth programs (focusing on MCs) ● developing portal and intranet ● developing document retention policy ● managing content (for web) ● designing inhouse ERP systems ● virtualizing teamwork (forums) engaging outside and inside experts: workshops,	● support from member countries ● increased management interest of need for knowledge and information management **AWARENESS** ● teamwork: within and cross departmental Examples: for OIL market projections PMAD and DSD; long term projections ESD has input from PMAD; refineries capacities (ie medium term) all departments work together ● attending more external meetings outside OPEC **COLLABORATION**

(side labels: COLLABORATION ; INDIVIDUAL STAKEHOLDER BEHAVIOR)

Exhibit 7: Illustration of axial coding for internal context in OPEC

CONTEXT: there is increasing complexity in the oil market, due to perceptions of the state of the industry, demand and supply security, and geopolitics (environment and sustainable development)

Casual conditions	Actions/interactions	Consequences
• government deregulation • high attrition rate in industry **ATTRITION** • global warming and climate change **SAFETY** • end of cheap oil (limits of growth) • negative public perceptions of oil industry • decreasing academic interest in oil industry • negative perception of job prospects in oil industry **PERCEPTIONS** • end of the cold war • sustainable development paradigm • environmental (EU green paper etc.) • litigation: NOPEC bill • MDG • globalisation • regional conflicts & terrorism **GEOPOLITICS** • energy demand security • energy supply security **SECURITY**	• revamping the OPEC database management systems to reflect the changes in environment: (new member country: Angola & new basket calculations) • redesigning the website • using live and ondemand webcast on the website • design of corporate identity, and unified look of presentations • designing and deploying a portal system and intranet • increased participation in international discussions on trade (WTO), environment (UNFCCC) and capacity building and technology transfer (Carbon sequestration) • engaging major producers and consumers of oil (EU-OPEC dialogue, OPEC-Russia dialogue etc) • creating the long term strategy • strengthening the secretariat: (consultants ideas and proposals) • organizing more international conferences and workshops • participating in JODI • interdepartmental projects and task forces (matrix management)	• increased access and use of OPEC portal for member countries and staff **INFORMATION ACCESS** • recognition of OPECs efforts to stabilize the oil market **RECOGNITION** • increased awareness of the position of OPEC on topical issues: renewable, climate change, taxation etc. • foras for creating win-win scenarios for addressing perceived double standards in energy policies • increased awareness of challenges facing developing countries in trade and environment "common but differentiated responsibilities" **AWARENESS** • increased stakeholder collaboration towards better producer/consumer understanding • increased awareness of the need for technical cooperation between the EU-OPEC • increased transparency (JODI) demand/ supply balance **COLLABORATION**

COLLABORATION / *INDIVIDUAL STAKEHOLDER BEHAVIOR*

Exhibit 8: Illustration of axial coding for external context in OPEC

Casual conditions	**Actions/interactions**	**Consequences**
• retirement of very experienced professionals **AGE PYRAMID**	• increased field operations, by over 2000% in the first 10 years.	• increased access and use of IRMA in field officers
• talent scarcity **RECRUITMENT**	• creating inhouse induction training for new recruits	• increased efficiency and timeliness of information dissemination and access **INFORMATION ACCESS**
• gaps in filling vacancies	• looking at cross cutting programs	• increased collaboration with other agencies
• statutory turnover	• developing portal strategy	• cultural diversity and method of approach **COLLABORATION**
• gaps in project overlap **SUCESSION**	• developing knowledge management strategy	• increased organizational awareness of need for managing human capital
• information sourcing	• management workshops on knowledge management	• increased management interest of need for collaboration and teamwork within the organization
• pockets of practices **REPORTING STRUCTURES**	• implementing document management systems (Doc.In)	• awareness of need for succession planning **AWARENESS**
• management concern with increasing the organizations ability to manage information and knowledge **COMPETENCY UPGRADE**	• developing guideline for field operations	
	• secure access to Integrated Resource Management system (IRMA) via yellow laptops	

CONTEXT: OSCE's top management look for better ways to consolidate and manage geographically dispersed information silos

INDIVIDUAL STAKEHOLDER BEHAVIOR — COLLABORATION — CAPACITY BUILDING

Exhibit 9: Illustration of axial coding for internal context in the OSCE

CONTEXT: Political perceptions on program revitalization, reform and rebalancing		
Casual conditions	**Actions/interactions**	**Consequences**
● International agreements, and charters on security in Europe ● end of cold war ● regional conflicts & terrorism ● increasing need for crisis management in Europe ● anti missile defence **GEOPOLITICS** ● NATO expansion ● EU expansion **COMPETITION** ● Political disagreements on the satisfactory delivery of dimensions of OSCE operations **PERCEPTION** ● Increasing number of programs without clear programmatic focus (overlap with NATO, UN, EU) ● increasing undocumented practices (from the CiO to the field operations)--need for better administration ● expansion of the OSCE programs and offices by over 2000% in just the first 10 years **MANDATE OVERLAP** ● pressure from member countries for better managed programs and political transparency REFORM	● seeking strategic partnerships with other security, humanitarian, reconstruction and aid communities ● codification of OSCE operational activities (planning and reporting) ● codification of the roles of OSCE leadership (particularly the CiO) ● explicit separation and monitoring of OSCE statements and agreement, from national statements by CiO and heads of missions, and OSCE institutions by press section and secretary general ● developing the Integrated resource and management system (IRMA) and "yellow laptop" ● developing the OSCE portal strategy ● participating in the international technology and crisis management (ITCM) conferences ● channeling economic and environmental services where they can have a "catalytic" role and lead to greater impact ● Articulating with the existing initiatives and efforts of a country and building on their strengths	● strategic partnerships ● issue leadership (election monitoring) ● recognizing strength of cultural diversity among recipient countries **COLLABORATION** ● increased access and use of IRMA and yellow laptop in field operations **INFORMATION ACCESS** ● recognition for OSCE **RECOGNITION** ● increased stakeholder awareness of need for better cooperation and synergy in politico-military and economic and enviromental policies **AWARENESS**
COLLABORATION		

Note: Left margin label: **CAPACITY BUILDING** *Right margin label:* **INDIVIDUAL STAKEHOLDER BEHAVIOR**

Exhibit 10: Illustration of axial coding for external context in the OSCE

CONTEXT: following the reform process, starting from 1997 to 1998 (UNIDO, 1997), UNIDO's top management looks for greater innovation from staff

Casual conditions	Actions/interactions	Consequences
● retirement of skilled professionals **AGE PYRAMID**	● downsizing—halved regular staff from 1400 to 700 (UNIDO, 1997)	● increased access and use of network to field officers
● talent scarcity (industrial development practitioners) **RECRUITMENT**	● creating mobility policy ● looking at cross cutting programs	● increased efficiency and timeliness of information dissemination (infobase portal) **INFORMATION ACCESS**
● gaps in filling vacancies ● gaps in project overlap **SUCESSION**	● recognizing teamwork (awards schemes) ● recruiting young professionals	● increased collaboration with other agencies ● leaner organization, with focused competencies
● information sourcing for timely evaluation of projects ● one man projects ● pockets of practices **REPORTING STRUCTURES**	● restructuring to encourage teamwork and communities of practices (ie. branches and units) ● youth programs (internships) ● developing portal (UNIDO exchange and infobase)	● recognizing strength of cultural diversity and method of approach **COLLABORATION** ● increased organizational awareness of need for managing human capital
● management concern with upgrading human capital to increase the ability to innovate **COMPETENCY UPGRADE**	● investigating digital archival systems (Archivista) ● developing technical corporation guidelines	● increased management interest of need for collaboration and teamwork within the organization
	● creating a bureau for organizational learning and strategy including independent evaluation group	● awareness of need for succession planning
	● secure token access to network	● lack of experience with results based approach. **AWARENESS**
	● developing quality criteria for benchmarking and classifying lessons learned	

CAPACITY BUILDING (left vertical label)

INDIVIDUAL STAKEHOLDER BEHAVIOR (right vertical label)

COLLABORATION

Exhibit 11: Illustration of axial coding for internal context in UNIDO

Casual conditions	Actions/interactions	Consequences
CONTEXT: increasing international pressure from member countries for better methods to define their needs, interests and priorities in technical cooperation programs		
● end of cold war	● seeking strategic partenerships with civil society organizations and, enterprises and firms.	● strategic partnerships
● less aid from soviet union		● issue leadership (global compact)
● liberalization of trade	● developing morandum of understanding with other international organizations	● integrated programs: recognizing strength of cultural diversity among recipient countries
● globalization and knowledge economy		
● terrorism and regional conflicts	● developing portal systems such as the UNIDO exchange and infobase	**COLLABORATION**
● millennium development goals		● increased access and use of UNIDO exchange and infobase worldwide
● corporate social responsibility of multinational corporations	● networking with academic and research institutions	
GEOPOLITICS	● developing the UNIDO institute	**INFORMATION ACCESS**
● increasing uncoordinated non UN multilateral donors	● chanelling services where they can have a catalytic role and lead to greater impact	● recognition for UNIDO's effectiveness by UK's Department for International Development (DFID)
● increasing earmarked contributions from non UN multilateral donors	● Articulating with the existing iniatives and efforts of a country and building on their strenghts	**RECOGNITION**
● rise of civil society organizations (CSOs)		● increased stakeholder awareness of need for better cooperation and synergy in development policies
COMPETITION		
● Political disagreements on the need for international intervention on industrialization		**AWARENESS**
PERCEPTION		
● Increasing number of UN funds and programs without clear programmatic focus		
MANDATE OVERLAP		
● pressure from member countries for better focused programs		
REFORM		

CAPACITY BUILDING · INDIVIDUAL STAKEHOLDER BEHAVIOR · **COLLABORATION**

Exhibit 12: Illustration of axial coding for external context in UNIDO

CONTEXT: UNODC starts to manage information systematically to improve transparency and increase efficiency

CAPACITY BUILDING

Casual conditions

- ageing and retirement of skilled management and professional staff

AGE PYRAMID

- statutory turnover
- UN charter (article 101)
- desirable range (staff quota)
- mobility policy
- gaps in filling vacancies
- gaps in project overlap

RECRUITMENT

- unmanaged processes & data
- decentralized IT

REPORTING STRUCTURES

- management concern with ensuring that organizational memory and transparency of processes and data

SUCCESSION

Actions/interactions

- developing the codification strategy ("all data is captured in the line of process")
- hiring armies of developers to try to codify and automate data and processes inhouse (workflow)
- investing heavily in technology
- developing integrated systems based on Lotus notes
- advertising and PR for new systems
- developing the PROFI portal and ERP system
- virtualizing teamwork, and investing in integrated messaging (skype, chat & messaging tools)
- abolishing non systematic workflows (paper)
- discouraging the use of personal drives to store data
- abolishing the use of Excel
- deploying redundant replicated systems in all 35 field offices
- retooling secretaries
- training managers on System

Consequences

- support from member countries due to increased transparency of UNODC activities
- awareness of staff number and contributions
- intensifying/formalizing codification strategy (no other way to work, but throuh system)

AWARENESS

- increased collaboration with government and international agents

COLLBORATION

- UN award the IT team in New York
- increased management support for codification strategy

RECOGNITION

- increased information access for MC and related government agents and institutions

INFORMATION ACCESS

INDIVIDUAL STAKEHOLDER BEHAVIOR

COLLABORATION

Exhibit 13: Illustration of axial coding for internal context in UNODC

CONTEXT: Need for better transparency in UNODC activities		
Casual conditions	**Actions/interactions**	**Consequences**
• concern for the future of the profession of international crime prevention, especially scientific research, publications and teaching, after the dissolution of the IPPC **ATTRITION** • human trafficking/slavery • increasing risk of chemical misuse (drug trafficking, bombs--terrorism) • exploitation of women and children (sexual, forced labour) **SAFETY** • lack of public awareness • lack of transparency for MC in UNODC TC funded activities **PERCEPTIONS** • end of the cold war • transnational organized crime • severe poverty • negative perception of job prospects **GEOPOLITICS** • threat of international terrorism **SECURITY**	• Organizing international congresses, commissions, conventions and treaties on crime, justice and treatment of offenders • increased cooperation with network of regional and international institutions (eg UN crime prevention and criminal justice program network) • assisting countries in elaboration and ratification and implementation (TC) of conventions and protocols • networking with academic institutions (e.g. via the international penal and penitentiary foundation) • providing Technical assistance for MCs to meet the UN global counter terrorism strategy	• increased access and use of PROFI system worldwide (used to monitor Technical assistance projects in real time) • Automating the project request process, using the Profi system **INFORMATION ACCESS** • winner of the UN 21 Commendation in the category of "process reengineering" for the ProFi (Programme and Financial Information Management) system **RECOGNITION** • increased awareness of need for better IT systems to tackle criminal issues **AWARENESS** • increased stakeholder collaboration towards better systems fo improve transparency • recognizing strength of cultural diversity and method of approach **COLLABORATION**

(Left margin: CAPACITY BUILDING; Right margin: INDIVIDUAL STAKEHOLDER BEHAVIOR; Bottom: COLLABORATION)

Exhibit 14: Illustration of axial coding for external context in UNODC

CONTEXT: EU (Austrian Presidency) focuses on sharing knowledge with European citizens		
Casual conditions	**Actions/interactions**	**Consequences**
● ageing and retirement of technical experts of council groups **AGE PYRAMID** ● talent scarcity at technical levels **RECRUITMENT** ● bureaucratic ● decentralized IT **REPORTING STRUCTURES** ● concern with ensuring that organizational memory is not lost when succeeding presidency takes over **SUCCESSION PLANNING**	● Austrian Presidency creates initiatives to rebuild confidence in Europe: "Europe listens", "Sound of Europe" (a debate on European identity), and the Café d' Europe ● looking at cross cutting programs and policies among member countries (security policy, agriculture policy etc) ● looks at long term strategic planning with other member countries (covering 3 years at a time) ● developing portals (the cafe Europe website, the Europe journal website, the Austrian presidency website etc) ● managing content ● virtualizing teamwork	● support from member countries **RECOGNITION** ● intensifying council groups meetings, consisting of country nationals, that will be familiar with dossier and delegates of other Member countries (and particularly Finland), so they can take over the presidency easily. **COLLABORATION** Increased awareness of the need to share knowledge horizontally between member countries governments and vertically to member country citizens. **AWARENESS** ● emails, secure portals, and websites **INFORMATION ACCESS**

CAPACITY BUILDING — **INDIVIDUAL STAKEHOLDER BEHAVIOR**

COLLABORATION

Exhibit 15: Illustration of axial coding for internal context in the EU

CONTEXT: growing opposition to the EU and its policies

CAPACITY BUILDING

Casual conditions	Actions/interactions	Consequences
• Unemployment • aging of population • job mobility • migration **ATTRITION** • negative public perceptions of EU as too bureaucratic and disconnected • negative perception of job prospects **PERCEPTIONS** • rejection of the EU constitutional treaty by France and Netherlands • low productivity and stagnation of economic growth in the EU • international development issues • election victory of Hamas • Iran nuclear dispute **GEOPOLITICS** • energy security • environmental issues • agriculture • EU enlargement **SECURITY** • threat of human trafficking • bird Flu • threat of drugs, crime and terrorism (Europol and Eurojust) **SAFETY**	• refocusing on the Lisbon strategy: "to make Europe, by 2010, the most competitive and the most dynamic knowledge-based economy in the world" •Support for the new Research Framework Program (FP7) and budget • initiating the "Europe is listening project" in light of serious communication deficits b/w EU and its citizens ie the rejection of the EU constitution etc. • focus on the Service Directive (service sector & SMEs) • Establishing the European Institute of Technology (qualifications normalization in EU) • organizing EU workshops at ministerial levels to discuss cross regional issues like: agriculture, environment, security, health, finance, transport and so on. • proposing the EU Green Paper • represent the EU in internal matters, example on energy: EU-OPEC and EU-Russia dialogues • planning for continuity of EU leadership, including Finland representatives (succeeding presidency) in all its high level activities technologies)	• increased information access through various portals and websites for EU citizens (the cafe Europe website, the Europe journal website, the Austrian presidency website etc) • Increased cross border collaboration (CORDIS, Europol, Eurojust) **INFORMATION ACCESS** • recognition of the efforts made of the Austrian Presidency: initiatives to rebuild confidence in Europe: "Europe listens", "Sound of Europe" (a debate on European identity), and the Café'e d' Europe **RECOGNITION** • increased trust and political agreement on sensitive issues (EU expansion, energy security etc.) and • increased awareness of need for knowledge sharing with EU citizens **AWARENESS** • increased collaboration with other European organizations like the Council of Europe on the Lisbon treaty • recognizing strength of cultural diversity **COLLABORATION**

INDIVIDUAL STAKEHOLDER BEHAVIOR

COLLABORATION

Exhibit 16: Illustration of axial coding for external context in the EU

REFERENCES

[1]   Webster, Merriam. *lookup for "revolution"* [online],
        Merriam-Webster Online Dictionary, Available from:
        http://www.m-w.com/dictionary/revolution [Accessed
        24 November 2006], 2005.

[2]   UNIDO. *Report of the external auditor, financial performance
        report and program performance report for the biennium 1998 -
        1999* [online], United Nations Industrial Development
        Organization, Available from:
        http://www.unido.org/userfiles/KayalarJ/16pbc4cor.pdf
        [Accessed 18 October 2006], 2000.

[3]   Hyde, Henry J. *United Nations Reform Act* [online], The
        Library of Congress, Available from:
        http://thomas.loc.gov/cgi-bin/query/z?c109:H.R.2745:
        [Accessed December 21 2006], 2005.

[4]   Stewart, Thomas A. *Intellectual Capital: The New Wealth of
        Organizations*. New York: Currency, 1998.

[5]   Hansen, M. T., N Nohria, and T. Tierney. *What's your
        strategy for managing knowledge*. Harvard Business Review,
        Vol. 77(1): p. 106-16, 1999.

[6]   Atreyi, Kankanhalli, et al. *The role of IT in successful
        knowledge management initiatives*. Communications of the
        ACM, Vol. 46(9): p. 69-73, 2003.

[7]   Jackson, Robert. *A study of the capacity of the United Nations
        development system* [online], Available from:

http://www.laetusinpraesens.org/docs/infwill/inf2.php [Accessed 16 August 2007], 1969.

[8]   The Nordic Project. *UN reform issues in the economic and social fields. A Nordic perspective.* Stockholm: Distributed by Almqvist & Wiksell International, p. 111, 1991.

[9]   Commission on Global Governance. *Our global neighborhood: the report of the Commission on Global Governance.* New york: Oxford university press, p. 410, 1995.

[10]   South Centre (South Commission). *For a strong and democratic United Nations: a South perspective on UN reform.* Geneva, Switzerland: South Centre, p. 229, 1996.

[11]   GPF. *UN Reform Chronology: 1992 - Present* [online], Global reform forum, Available from: http://www.globalpolicy.org/reform/intro/chronology. htm [Accessed 31 August 2007], 2006.

[12]   Annan, Kofi A. *Renewing the United Nations: A program for reform, addressed to the General Assembly* [online], United Nations Secretariat, Available from: http://www.un.org/reform/pdfs/1997%20renewing%20t he%20un-prog%20for%20reform.pdf [Accessed 23 August 2006], 1997.

[13]   Magarinos, Carlos. *Economic development and UN reform.* Vienna, Austria: United Nations Industrial Development Organization (UNIDO), 2005.

[14]   Magarinos, Carlos , et al. *Reforming the UN System: UNIDO's Need Driven Model.* the Hague: Kluwer Law International, 2001.

[15]   Greenpeace. *Former Environmental Ministers call on UN to*
         reform IAEA mandate and End the Nuclear Age [online],
         Green Peace International, Available from:
         http://www.greenpeace.org/international/press/release
         s/former-environmental-ministers [Accessed 16 October
         2006], 2006.

[16]   Norway. *Reform of the OSCE* [online], The permanent
         delegation to the OSCE, Vienna, Available from:
         http://www.norway-
         osce.org/current/admreform/reformofosce.htm
         [Accessed 16 October 2006], 2004.

[17]   Slovenia. *Vajgl Calls for OSCE Reform* [online],
         Government Public Relations and Media Office, republic
         of Slovenia, Available from:
         http://www.uvi.si/eng/slovenia/publications/slovenia-
         news/1319/1324/ [Accessed 16 October 2006], 2004.

[18]   Annan, Kofi. *Investing in the United Nations For a Stronger*
         Organization Worldwide [online], United Nations, Available
         from: http://www.un.org/reform/ [Accessed 16 October
         2006], 2004.

[19]   Anderson, Kym. *Lobbying Incentives and the Pattern of*
         Protection in Rich and Poor Countries. Economic
         Development and Cultural Change, Vol. 43(2): p. 401,
         1995.

[20]   Deen, Thalif. *Rich vs. Poor in Power Struggle, Says Top UN*
         Official [online], Global Policy Forum, Available from:
         http://www.globalpolicy.org/reform/topics/manage/20
         06/0531struggle.htm [Accessed 16 October 2006], 2006.

[21]   CEB. *Summary of the High-level Committee on Programs*
         (HLCP) retreat held at the Greentree Foundation in Manhasset,
         New York, from 19 to 21 July 2005 [online], UN System
         Chief Executive Board for Communication, Available

from:
http://ceb.unsystem.org/hlcp/documents/Session.Repor
ts/ceb-2005-6.pdf [Accessed 23 July 2006], 2005.

[22]   Alighieri, Dante. *On World Government (De Monarchia)*. 2d
        rev. ed. ed. New York: Macmillan Pub Co, 1957.

[23]   Kant, Emanuel. *Eternal Peace and other international Essays*.
        Boston MA: World Peace Foundation, 1914.

[24]   Rochester, J. M. *The rise and fall of international organization
        as a field of study*. International Organization, Vol. 40(4): p.
        777-813, 1986.

[25]   Meadows, Donella H., Jorgen Randers, and Dennis L.
        Meadows. *Limits to growth*. Vermont: Chelsea Green
        Publishing Company, 2004.

[26]   Shah, Sonia. *Crude: The Story of Oil*. New York: Seven
        Stories Press, 2006.

[27]   Goodrich, Leland M. and Charles E. Putman. *International
        Organization Politics and Process*. Wisconsin: Univ. of
        Wisconsin Press, 1973.

[28]   Potter, Pitman B. *Classification of international
        organizations*. the American Political Science Review, Vol.
        29(2): p. 212-224, 1935.

[29]   Oxford Reference, Online. *1st results from online search for
        "international organization"* [online], Oxford University
        Press, Available from: http://www.oxfordreference.com
        [Accessed 28 July 2006], 2006.

[30]   Plano, Jack C. and Roy Olton. *The International Relations
        Dictionary*. Vol. 4th edition ABC-Clio Inc., 1988.

[31]   Winstanley, D. D., S. Sorabij, and S. Darwson. *When the pieces don't fit: a stakeholder power matrix to analyze public sector restructuring*. Public Money and Management, Vol. 15(2): p. 19-26, 1995.

[32]   OPEC. *OPEC Long-Term Strategy* [online], OPEC Secretariat, Available from: http://www.opec.org/library/Special%20Publications/p df/OPECLTS.pdf [Accessed 16 March 2006], 2005.

[33]   Bergesen, Helge Ole and Leiv Lunde. *Dinosaurs or Dynamos? The United Nations and the World Bank at the turn of the Century*. London: Earthscan Publications, 1999.

[34]   UNIDO. *UNIDO's Thematic Priorities* [online], United Nations Industrial Development Organization, Available from: http://www.unido.org/doc/51918 [Accessed 22 August 2005], 2005.

[35]   OSCE. *The Organization for Security and Co-operation in Europe* [online], The Organization for Security and Co-operation in Europe, Available from: http://www.osce.org/ [Accessed 29 August 2006], 2006.

[36]   Blackler, F. *Knowledge, knowledge work and organizations: an overview and interpretation*. Organizational Studies, Vol. 16(6): p. 1021-46, 1995.

[37]   Star, S. L. and J. R. Griesemer. *Institutional Ecology 'Translations' and Boundary Objects: Amateurs and Professionals in Berkeley's Museum of Vertebrate Zoology 1907-39*. Social Studies of Science, Vol. 19(3): p. 387-420, 1989.

[38]   Ackerman, M. and C. Halverson. *Organizational memory: processes, boundary objects and trajectories*. In Proceedings of the 32nd Annual Hawaii International Conference on System Sciences. Maui, Hi: IEEE, p. 43-55, 1999.

[39]   Briers, M. and W. F. Chua. *The role of actor-networks and boundary objects in management accounting change: a field study of an implementation of activity-based costing.* Accounting, Organizations and Society, Vol. 23(3): p. 237-269, 2001.

[40]   Pawlowski, S.D. and D Robey. *Bridging User Organizations: Knowledge Brokering and the Work of Information Technology professionals.* MIS quarterly, Vol. 28(4): p. 645-672, 2004.

[41]   Zack, M. H. *If Managing Knowledge is the solution, then what is the problem?*, in *Knowledge management and business model innovation* Y. Malhotra, Editor, Idea Group Publishing: Hershey, PA, 2000.

[42]   CCPOQ. *Knowledge Management and Information Technology* [online], 17th Session of the Consultative Committee on Program and Operational Questions (CCPOQ), Available from: http://www.unssc.org/web1/programmes/km/documents/crp-14.pdf [Accessed 22 July 2006], 2000.

[43]   Gallupe, Brent. *Knowledge management systems: surveying the landscape.* International Journal of management Reviews, Vol. 3(1): p. 61-77, 2001.

[44]   UN. *Charter of the United Nations* [online], United Nations, Available from: http://www.un.org/aboutun/charter/ [Accessed 26 July 2006], 1945.

[45]   UN. *Millennium Development Goals* [online], United Nations, Available from: http://www.un.org/millenniumgoals/ [Accessed 18 January 2007], 2000.

[46]   UN. *History of the UN charter: The declaration of St. James Palace* [online], United Nations, Available from:

http://www.un.org/aboutun/charter/history/ [Accessed 7 July 2007], 2005.

[47]   Hazlitt, Henry. *Economics in One Lesson: The Shortest and Surest Way to Understand Basic Economics.* New York: Three Rivers Press, 1988.

[48]   UNFCCC. *Parties to the Kyoto Protocol* [online], United Nations Framework Convention on Climate Change, Available from: http://maindb.unfccc.int/public/country.pl?group=kyot o [Accessed 24 July 2007], 2007.

[49]   Hasenclever, Andreas, Peter Mayer, and Volker Rittberger. *Interests, Power, Knowledge: The study of international regimes.* Mershon International Studies Review, Vol. (40): p. 177-228, 1996.

[50]   Huysman, Marleen. *Design requirements for knowledge-sharing tools: a need for social capital analysis,* in *Social Capital and information technology,* M. Huysman and V. Wulf, Editors, MIT Press: Cambridge, 2004.

[51]   ACC. *Summary of conclusions of the Administrative Committee on coordination at its second regular session of 1997* [online], Administrative Committee on Coordination, Available from: http://ceb.unsystem.org/documents/summary.conclusio ns/9801921e.pdf [Accessed 1 August 2006], 1997.

[52]   ACC. *ACC Statement on Universal Access to Basic Communication and Information Services (1997)* [online], UNITeS, Available from: http://www.unites.org/html/resource/acc1997.htm [Accessed 1 August 2006], 1997.

[53]   Zack, M. H. and J. L. McKenny. *Social context and integration in ongoing computer-supported management*

groups., in *Knowledge, groupware and the internet*, D.E. Smith, Editor, Butterworth-Heinemann: Boston, 2000.

[54]   Hedlund, G. *A model of Knowledge Management and the N-Form Corporation.* Strategic Management Journal, Vol. 15(Special Issue): p. 73-90, 1994.

[55]   Davenport, Thomas H. and Laurence Prusak. *Working Knowledge: how organizations manage what they know*: Harvard Business School Press p. 240, 2000.

[56]   Swan, J., et al. *Knowledge Management and Innovation: Networks and Networking.* Journal of knowledge Management, Vol. 3(4): p. 262-275, 1999.

[57]   Alavi, M and D. E. Leidner. *Knowledge management and knowledge management systems: conceptual foundations and research issues.* MIS quarterly, Vol. 25(1): p. 107-136, 2001.

[58]   Spender, J. C. *An Overview: What's new and important about knowledge management? Building new bridges between Managers and Academics*, in *Managing Knowledge*, S. Little and T. Ray, Editors, Sage: London, 2005.

[59]   Sveiby, K. *What is Knowledge Management* [online], Sveiby knowledge Associates, Available from: http://www.sveiby.com/Portals/0/articles/Knowledge Management.html [Accessed 23 August 2006], 2001.

[60]   Stewart, Thomas A. *Brainpower*, in *Fortune*. p. 42-60, 1991.

[61]   Bontis, Nick. *Managing Organizational Knowledge by diagnosing Intellectual Capital: Framing and Advancing the state of the Field.* International Journal of Technology, Vol. 18(5-5): p. 433-462, 1999.

[62]   Nahapiet, J. and S. Ghoshal. *Social Capital, Intellectual Capital and organizational advantage*. Academy of Management Review, Vol. 23(2): p. 242-266, 1998

[63]   Carlolis, Donna Marie De. *The Role of Social Capital and Organizational Knowledge in Enhancing Entrepreneurial Opportunities in High-Technology Environments*, in *The Strategic Management of Intellectual Capital and Organizational Knowledge*, C.W. Choo and N. Bontis, Editors, Oxford University Press: New York. p. 699-709, 2002.

[64]   Choo, Chun Wei and Nick Bontis. *The Strategic Management of Intellectual Capital and Organizational Knowledge*. New York: Oxford University Press, 2002.

[65]   ICS. *Words of value – an IC dictionary* [online], Intellectual Capital Services (ICS) Ltd., Available from: http://www.intcap.com/ICS_Article_2003_Words_of_Val ue_An_IC_Dictionary.pdf [Accessed 12 January 2006], 2002.

[66]   Arthur, W Brian. *Increasing Returns and path dependence in the economy*. Michigan: Univ. of Michigan Press, 1994.

[67]   Romer, Paul M. *Two strategies for economic development: using ideas and producing ideas*. In The World Bank annual conference on development economics: World Bank, 1993.

[68]   Polanyi, Michael. *The Tacit Dimension*. Garden City, NY: Doubleday, 1966.

[69]   Cook, S. D. N. and J. S. Brown. *Bridging Epistemologies: The Generative dance between Organizational Knowledge and Organizational Knowing*. Organizational Science, Vol. 10(4): p. 381-400, 1999.

[70]   Nonaka, I., R. Toyama, and N. Konno. *SECI, Ba and leadership: a unified Model of Dynamic Knowledge Creation.* Long Range Planning, Vol. 33(1): p. 5-34, Edited version, 2000.

[71]   Nonaka, I. and Takeuchi. *The knowledge-creating company: How Japanese companies create the dynamics of innovation.* Oxford: Oxford University Press, 1995.

[72]   Borghoff, U. M. and R. (Eds) Pareschi. *Information Technology for Knowledge Management.* Berlin: Springer-Verlag, 1998.

[73]   Drucker, P. F. *The age of discontinuity: guidelines to our changing society.* London: Heinemann, 1969.

[74]   Skyrme, D. J. and D. M. Amidon. *Creating the knowledge based business.* London: Business Intelligence limited, 1997.

[75]   Taylor, Frederick Winslow. *The Principles of Scientific Management.* (First Published in 1911) New York: Dover Publications, p. 76, 1998.

[76]   CEB. *Development of general service/ professional staff ratio* [online], Chief Executives Board for Coordination, Available from: http://hr.unsystemceb.org/statistics/analysis/stats/2004/4A4B [Accessed 19 July 2007], 2004.

[77]   Ruggles, Rudy L. *Knowledge Management Tools.* Oxford: Butterworth-Heinemann, 1997.

[78]   Olha, Bondarenko and Janssen Ruud. *Documents at Hand: Learning from Paper to Improve Digital Technologies,* in *Proceedings of the SIGCHI conference on Human factors in computing systems,* ACM Press: Portland, Oregon, USA, 2005.

[79]   Ruggles, R. *Knowledge Tools: using technology to manage knowledge better. Working paper*, Ernst and Young, 1997.

[80]   Wensley, Anthony K.P. . *Tools for Knowledge management* [online], Available from: http://www.icasit.org/km/resources/toolsforkm.htm [Accessed 28 August 2006], 2001.

[81]   AIIM. *What is ECM?* [online], Association for Information and Image Management, Available from: http://www.aiim.org/ [Accessed 29 December 2006], 2006.

[82]   Wikipedia. *Enterprise resource planning* [online], Wikipedia, Available from: http://en.wikipedia.org/wiki/Enterprise_resource_plann ing [Accessed 29 December 2006], 2006.

[83]   Coleman. *Social Capital in the creation of human capital.* American Journal of Sociology, Vol. 94: p. S95-S120, 1988.

[84]   Koka, B. R. and J. E. Prescott. *Strategic alliances as social capital: a multidimensional view.* Strategic Management Journal, Vol. 23(9): p. 795-816, 2002.

[85]   Adler, P.S and S. W. Kwon. *Social capital: Prospects for a new concept.* Academy of Management Review, Vol. 27(1): p. 17-40, 2002.

[86]   Bourdieu, P. and L. J. D. Wacquant. *An invitation to reflexive sociology.* Chicago: University of Chicago Press, 1992.

[87]   Putnam. *Bowling alone: Americas declining social capital.* Annual review of sociology, Vol. 24: p. 1-24, 1995.

[88]   UN. *The Millenium Development Goals Report* [online],
        United Nations, Available from:
        http://mdgs.un.org/unsd/mdg/Resources/Static/Produ
        cts/Progress2006/MDGReport2006.pdf [Accessed 27
        November 2006], 2006.

[89]   Prusak, Larry. *The knowledge Advantage*. Strategy and
        Leadership, Vol. 24(2): p. 6-8, 1996.

[90]   Brandenburger, Adam M. and Barry J. Nalebuff. *Co-
        Opetition*. New York: Doubleday, 1997.

[91]   Morgenstern, Oskar and John Von Neumann. *Theory of
        Games and Economic Behavior* Princeton, NJ: Princeton
        University Press, 1980.

[92]   Smith, Jackie. *Globalizing Resistance: The Battle of Seattle
        and the Future of Social Movements*. Vol. 6(1): p. 1 - 19, 2001

[93]   Annan, Kofi. *The Nobel Prize: Noble Lecture* [online], Nobel
        foundation, Available from:
        http://nobelprize.org/nobel_prizes/peace/laureates/200
        1/annan-lecture.html [Accessed 24 July 2007], 2001.

[94]   Strauss, A. and J. Corbin. *Basics of Qualitative Research*.
        Newbury Park, Carlifornia: Sage Publications, 1990.

[95]   Glaser, Barney G. *Theoretical sensitivity*. Mill Valley,
        California: Sociology press, 1978.

[96]   IAEA. *Statute* [online], IAEA, Available from:
        http://www.iaea.org/About/statute.html [Accessed 5
        July 2005], 1956.

[97]   IMO. *IMO: what it is, what it does and how it works* [online],
        International Maritime Organization, Available from:

http://www.imo.org/About/mainframe.asp?topic_id=32
5 [Accessed 9 July 2007], 2002.

[98]   IMO. *Strategic Plan and High Level Action Plan* [online],
       International Maritime Organization, Available from:
       http://www.imo.org/About/mainframe.asp?topic_id=88
       8 [Accessed 18 August 2007], 2006.

[99]   EU. *One year after the Prestige disaster, the Commission*
       publishes the first list of ships definitively banned from EU
       ports [online], EU Commission, Available from:
       http://europa.eu/rapid/pressReleasesAction.do?referenc
       e=IP/03/1547&format=HTML&aged=1&language=EN&g
       uiLanguage=en [Accessed 7 August 2007], 2003.

[100] Mitropoulos, Efthimios. *Speech: Challenges for the*
       international maritime organization in the 21st century
       [online], International Maritime Organization, Available
       from:
       http://www.imo.org/Safety/mainframe.asp?topic_id=84
       7&doc_id=3741 [Accessed 18 August 2007], 2004.

[101] WMU. *World Maritime University: Introduction* [online],
       World Maritime University, Available from:
       http://www.wmu.se/Pages/PageTemplate_1.asp?Section
       Id=828 [Accessed 10 July 2007], 2001.

[102] IMLI. *About Us* [online], International maritime law
       institute, Available from:
       http://www.imli.org/about.htm [Accessed 10 July 2007],
       2001.

[103] OFID. *Heavily Indebted Poor Countries Initiative*, in *OFID*
       Annual Report 1999, OPEC fund for international
       development: Vienna. p. 35, 1999.

[104] OFID. *Cooperating partners* [online], OPEC fund for
       international development, Available from:

http://www.opecfund.org/about/cooperating.aspx
[Accessed 16 July 2007], 2007.

[105]   OPEC. *World Oil Outlook* [online], Organization of the
         Petroleum Exporting Countries, Available from:
         http://www.opec.org/library/World%20Oil%20Outlook/
         pdf/WorldOilOutlook.pdf [Accessed July 23 2007], 2007.

[106]   EU. *A European Strategy for Sustainable, Competitive and
         Secure Energy* [online], EU Commission, Available from:
         http://ec.europa.eu/energy/green-paper-
         energy/doc/2006_03_08_gp_document_en.pdf [Accessed
         11 July 2007], 2006.

[107]   USA. *National Energy Policy* [online], US Government,
         Available from:
         http://www.whitehouse.gov/energy/National-Energy-
         Policy.pdf [Accessed 11 July 2007], 2001.

[108]   OPEC. *Who gets what from oil?* [online], Organization of
         the Petroleum Exporting countries, Available from:
         http://www.opec.org/library/Special%20Publications/p
         df/WGW2007.pdf [Accessed 11 July 2007], 2007.

[109]   OPEC. *"OPEC Statute" The original text of the
         Organization's Statute was approved by the Conference in
         January 1961 in Caracas — Resolution II.6.* [online], OPEC,
         Available from:
         http://www.opec.org/library/opec%20statute/pdf/os.p
         df [Accessed January 01, 2006], 2001.

[110]   Hamel, Mohamed. *OPEC: Dialogue between Producers and
         Consumers* [online], Organization of the petroleum
         Exporting Countries, Available from:
         http://www.opec.org/opecna/Speeches/2007/DialogueP
         rodCons.htm [Accessed 11 July 2007], 2007.

[111]   OPEC. *EU-OPEC Roundtable on Energy Policies* [online], Organization of the petroleum exporting countries, Available from: http://www.opec.org/opecna/Press%20Releases/2007/O PECEUroundtable.htm [Accessed 23 July 2007], 2007.

[112]   Pitner, Tomas, et al. *Web 2.0 as platform for inclusive universal access in cooperative learning and knowledge sharing.* In Proceedings of the 7th International Conference on Knowledge Management (IKnow 07). Graz: Journal of Universal Computer Science, September 5-7, 2007.

[113]   Zellner, Wolfgang. *Managing change in Europe.* Hamburg: Center for OSCE Research, Institute for peace research and security policy at the University of Hamburg, 2005.

[114]   OSCE. *Tenth Meeting of the Ministerial Council (6 and 7 December 2002)* [online], Organization for Security and Co-operation in Europe, Available from: http://www.osce.org/documents/mcs/2002/12/4174_en. pdf [Accessed 15 July 2007], 2002.

[115]   Vision paper: Management of Information and knowledge. *Vision paper: Management of Information and knowledge.* Vienna: Department of Management and Finance, OSCE, 2004.

[116]   UNIDO. *Strategic Guidelines--towards improved UNIDO program delivery* [online], United Nations Industrial Development, Available from: http://www.unido.org/file-storage/download/?file_id=11059 [Accessed 9 November 2006], 2003.

[117]   UNODC. *Crime Prevention and Criminal Justice* [online], United Nations Office on Drugs and Crime, Available from:

http://www.unodc.org/unodc/en/crime_prevention.htm
l [Accessed 23 July 2007], 2007.

[118]   UNODC. *Programme and Financial Information Management*
         System [online], United Nations Office on Drugs and
         Crime, Available from:
         http://www.unodc.org/pdf/missions/info_profi_missio
         ns.pdf [Accessed 18 July 2007], 2005.

[119]   EU. *Multiannual strategic programme (2004-2006)* [online],
         Council (General Affairs and External Relations),
         Available from:
         http://www.eu2006.fi/the_presidency/en_GB/strategic_
         programme/_files/75301786116294090/default/st15896.e
         n03.pdf [Accessed 7 August 2007], 2003.

[120]   EU. *Lisbon European Council 23 and 24 March 2000:*
         Presidency Conclusions [online], European Council,
         Available from:
         http://www.europarl.europa.eu/summits/lis1_en.htm
         [Accessed 4 June 2007], 2000.

[121]   EU. *Glossary: Lisbon Strategy* [online], European
         Commission, Available from:
         http://europa.eu/scadplus/glossary/lisbon_strategy_en.
         htm [Accessed 9 July 2007], 2000.

[122]   EU. *Press Release: Council approves EU research programmes*
         for 2007-2013 [online], COUNCIL OF THE EUROPEAN
         UNION, Available from:
         http://www.consilium.europa.eu/ueDocs/cms_Data/doc
         s/pressData/en/misc/92236.pdf [Accessed 18 October
         2007], 2006.

[123]   Child, John. *trust and International Strategic Alliances*, in
         Trust within and between organizations, C. Lane and R.
         Bachmann, Editors, Oxford University Press: New York,
         1998.

[124] Mitchell, Ronald B. *Sources of transparency: Information systems in international regimes.* International Studies Quarterly, Vol. 42: p. 109-130, 1998.

[125] IMO. *IMO Technical cooperation programme* [online], International Maritime Organization, Available from: http://194.196.162.45/TCD/mainframe.asp?topic_id=27 [Accessed October 20, 2007], 1991.

[126] Answers.com. *Bush Doctrine* [online], Answers.com, Available from: http://www.answers.com/topic/bush-doctrine [Accessed October 20, 2007]

[127] Lewicki, R. J. and B. B Buknker. *Developing and maintaining trust in work relations,* in *Trust in organizations,* Kramer and Tyler, Editors. p. 114-139, 1996.

[128] Kotter, John P. *What leaders really do.* Boston, MA: Harvard Business School, 1999.

[129] Lebow, Rob and William L. Simon. *Lasting Change: the shared values process that makes companies great.* NY: John Wiley & Sons, 1997.

[130] IAEA. *Managing nuclear knowledge: strategies and human resource development.* In Proceedings of the International conference on managing nuclear knowledge: strategies and human resource development. Saclay, France: International Atomic Energy Agency, 2004.

[131] IAEA. *Strategic thinking on the Agency's role in NKM,* in *Nuclear Information and Knowledge,* INIS & NKM section, IAEA: Vienna, 2005.

[132] IAEA. *School for Nuclear Knowledge Management* [online], International Atomic Energy Agency, Available from:

http://www.iaea.org/inisnkm/nkm/pages/NKM_Trieste Italy_2006.htm [Accessed 21 March 2007], 2007.

[133]   GEF. *Implementing Agencies* [online], Global Environment Facility, Available from: http://www.gefweb.org/Partners/Exe_Agencies/exe_ag encies.html [Accessed 17 November 2006], 1991.

[134]   GEF. *Executing Agencies* [online], Global Environment Facility, Available from: http://www.gefweb.org/Partners/Exe_Agencies/exe_ag encies.html [Accessed 17 November 2006], 1991.

[135]   Morgan, G. *images of Organizations*. Thousand Oaks, CA: Sage, 1997.

[136]   Bodeau, D. J. *A conceptual model for computer security risk analysis*, in *Proceedings of the 8th annual computer security application*, IEEE. p. 55-63, 1992.

[137]   Anderson, E., J. Choobineh, and M.R. Grimaila. *An Enterprise Level Security Requirements Specification Model*. In Proceedings of the 38th Annual Hawaii International Conference on System Sciences (HICSS 05). Hawaii: IEEE, 2005.

[138]   I2SF. *Generally accepted System Security principles (GASSP)* [online], International Information System Security Foundation, Available from: http://www.infosectoday.com/Articles/gassp.pdf [Accessed 16 August 2007]

[139]   Calabro, Aurelia. *Business Plan for Ethiopia's leather and leather products industry* [online], United Nations Induatrial Development Organization, Available from: http://www.unido.org/doc/40823 [Accessed 22 October 2007], 2005.

[140]   Wenger, E. *Communities of Practice: Learning, Meaning and Identity* New York: Cambridge University Press, 1998.

[141]   Wenger, Etienne. *Communities of practice and social learning systems*, in *Knowing in Organizations: A Practice-based Approach*, D. Nicolini, Gheradi, S. and Yanow, D, Editor, M. E. Sharpe: New York, 2003.

[142]   DoD. *5015.2-STD: Design criteria standard for electronic records management software applications* [online], US Department of Defense, Available from: http://jitc.fhu.disa.mil/recmgt/p50152s2.pdf [Accessed 18 May 2007], 2002.

[143]   Holsapple, C. W. and K Jones. *Exploring primary activities of the knowledge chain*. Knowledge and management, Vol. 11(3): p. 155-174, 2004.

[144]   Holsapple, C. W. and M Singh. *The knowledge chain model: activities for competitiveness*. Expert Systems with Applications, Vol. 20(1): p. 77-89, 2001.

[145]   Porter, M. E. *Competitive Strategy*. New York: The free press, 1980.

[146]   Jordan, B, R Goldman, and A Eichler. *A technology for supporting knowledge work: the reptool*, in *Information Technology for Knowledge Management*, U.M. Borghoff and R. Pareschi, Editors, Springer-Verlag: Berlin, 1998.

[147]   OSCE. *OSCE Mission in Kosovo* [online], The Organization for Security and Co-operation in Europe, Available from: http://www.osce.org/kosovo/ [Accessed 25 March 2007], 2007.

[148]   Krasner, Stephen D. *Structural causes and regime consequences: regimes as intervening variables.*, in

International regimes, S.d. krasner, Editor, Cornell Univ. press: Ithaca, NY. p. 1-21, 1983.

[149]   Mearsheimer, John. *The tragedy of great power politics*. New York: W. W. Norton & Company, 2001.

[150]   JODI. *About JODI* [online], International Energy Forum (IEF), Available from: http://www.jodidata.org/FileZ/introduction.htm#_A_Sh ort_Background [Accessed 15 August 2005], 2001.

[151]   MOREQ. *Model requirements for the management of electronic records* [online], European commission, Available from: http://www.digitaleduurzaamheid.nl/bibliotheek/docs/ moreq.pdf [Accessed 5 July 2007], 2001.

[152]   NAA. *Organizing business information* [online], National Archives of Australia, Available from: http://www.naa.gov.au/recordkeeping/control/tools/ch pt1.html [Accessed 26 August 2007], 2001.

[153]   UNIDO. *Former organizational structures* [online], United Nations Industrial Development Organization, Available from: http://www.unido.org/file-storage/download/?file_id=60711 [Accessed 26 August 2007], 2007.

[154]   Kennedy and Schauder. *Records Management: A Guide to Corporate Recordkeeping*. 2nd edition ed. Longmans, Melbourne, p. 115, 1998.

[155]   DIRKS. *DIRKS manual - Step B: A strategic Approach to managing business information*. Australia: National archives of Australia, 2001.

[156]   Johnson, G and K Scholes. *Exploring corporate strategy*. 3rd edn ed. Englewood Clifs, NJ: Prentice-Hall, 1993.

[157]   Klischewski, Ralf. *Towards an ontology for e-document management in public administration--the case of Schleswig-Holstein*. In Proceedings of the 36th Hawaii International Conference on System sciences (HICSS'03). Waikoloa, Hawaii: IEEE Computer Society, 2003.

[158]   Snidal, Duncan. *The game theory of international politics*. World Politics, Vol. 38(1): p. 25-57, 1985.

[159]   Pike, Dr. Steve and Ind. Prof. Göran Roos. *Intellectual Capital Measurement and Holistic Value Approach* [online], Available from: http://www.intcap.com/downloads/ICS_Article_2000_IC_Measurement_HVA.pdf [Accessed 2 April 2005], 2000.

[160]   Ugbor, Ugo and Carlos Chanduvi-Suarez. *Becoming knowledge Focused: Developing a practice for managing knowledge in international organizations*. In Proceedings of the 7th International Conference on Knowledge Management (IKnow 07). Graz, Austria: Journal of Universal Computer Science, 2007.

[161]   Sveiby, K. *The New Organizational Wealth: Managing and Measuring Knowledge Based Assets*. San Fransisco: Berrett-Koehler, 2001.

[162]   Rumelt, R.P. *Towards a strategic theory of the firm*, in *Competitive Strategic Management*, R.B. Lamb, Editor, Prentice Hall: New Jersey. p. 556-570, 1984.

[163]   Wernerfelt, B. *A resource-based view of the firm*. Strategic Management Journal, Vol. 5: p. 171-180, 1984.

[164]   Dierickx, I. and K. Cool. *Asset stock accumulation and sustainability of competitive advantage*. Management Science, Vol. 35(12): p. 1504-1511, 1989.

[165]   Barney, J. B. *Firm resources and sustained competitive advantage.* Journal of Management, Vol. 17(1): p. 99-120, 1991.

[166]   Hall, R. *A framework linking intangible resources and capabilities to sustainable competitive advantage.* Strategic Management Journal, Vol. (14): p. 607-618, 1993.

[167]   Lambert, Youry. *The United Nations Industrial Development Organization : UNIDO and problems of international economic cooperation.* Westport, CT Greenwood Publishing Group, Inc., 1993.

[168]   IMO. *International Convention for the Prevention of Pollution from Ships (MARPOL)* [online], International Maritime Organization, Available from: http://www.imo.org/Conventions/contents.asp?doc_id=678&topic_id=258 [Accessed 10 July 2007], 1978.

[169]   Strauss, A. and J. Corbin. *Grounded theory methodology: An overview.* , in *Handbook of Qualitative Research*, N. Denzin and Y. Lincoln, Editors, Sage: Thousand Oaks CA, 1994.

www.ingramcontent.com/pod-product-compliance
Lightning Source LLC
Chambersburg PA
CBHW041308210326
41599CB00003B/23